ARISTOTLE ON FRIENDSHIP

ARISTOTLE

ON

FRIENDSHIP

Being an expanded translation
of the

NICOMACHEAN ETHICS

BOOKS VIII & IX

by

GEOFFREY PERCIVAL

CAMBRIDGE
AT THE UNIVERSITY PRESS
1940

CAMBRIDGE
UNIVERSITY PRESS

University Printing House, Cambridge CB2 8BS, United Kingdom

Cambridge University Press is part of the University of Cambridge.

It furthers the University's mission by disseminating knowledge in the pursuit of education, learning and research at the highest international levels of excellence.

www.cambridge.org
Information on this title: www.cambridge.org/9781107497719

© Cambridge University Press 1940

First published 1940
First paperback edition 2015

A catalogue record for this publication is available from the British Library

ISBN 978-1-107-49771-9 Paperback

ΦΙΛΟΙΣ ΤΟΚΕΥΣΙ

CONTENTS

PREFACE

The aim of this edition is to present in as complete a form as possible the argument of Books VIII and IX of the *Nicomachean Ethics*. The method of the edition is explained in the second section of the Introduction.

I give a brief bibliography of those works which have been of assistance to me: these deal in the main with the literature bearing on friendship in the life and thought of Greece before Aristotle. The published literature on the *Ethics* is, in the main, public property: and a complete bibliography is to be found in the Teubner edition of Apelt. Mr Rackham gives a brief account of the more recent editions which have appeared in English, in the preface to his Loeb edition of the *Nicomachean Ethics*.

I owe a good deal to the careful analysis to which Mr Rackham has submitted the text: and also to the translation of Dr Ross. My thanks are due to Professor Cornford, who supervised my research: his kindly consideration, and the stimulus of his conversation, have been of great help to me. Mr L. H. G. Greenwood, of Emmanuel College, Cambridge, has always been ready to give me the benefit of his advice: and no work of mine would be complete without an acknowledgement of the inspiration which I have derived from his teaching and his encouragement.

My thanks are also due to the Syndics of the University Press, who have generously undertaken to bear the cost of publishing this work.

G. P.

December
1939

BIBLIOGRAPHY

ARNIM, H. VON. *Platos Jugenddialoge*. Leipzig, 1914.

BRINK, K. O. *Stil und Form der pseudaristotelische Magna Moralia*. Diss. Munich, 1931.

CARRAU, L. *Aristote, Morale à Nicomaque*, Livre VIII. Paris, 1881.
CHASE, A. H. *Quomodo amicitiam tractaverint tragici Graeci quaeritur*. Diss. Harvard, 1929. (See *Harvard Studies in Classical Philology*, vol. XLI, 1930, pp. 186–189.)
CORNFORD, F. M. *Plato's Theory of Knowledge*. Kegan Paul, 1935.
— *Plato's Cosmology*. Kegan Paul, 1937.
CURTIUS, E. 'Die Freundschaft im Alterthume.' In *Alterthume und Gegenwart*, I, 1882$^{(3)}$, pp. 183–202.

DELATTE, A. *Études sur la littérature Pythagoricienne*. Bibliothèque de l'école des hautes études, 217. Paris, 1915.
DIELS, E. *Die Fragmente der Vorsokratiker*. 3rd edition.
DIRLMEIER, F. φίλος und φιλία im vorhellenistischen Griechentum. Diss. Munich, 1931.
DITTMAR, H. *Aeschines von Sphettus*. Berlin, 1912. (Philologische Unter suchungen, vol. XXI.)
DUGAS, L. *L'amitié antique*. Paris, 1894.

EARP, F. R. *The way of the Greeks*. O.U. Press, 1929.
EERNSTMANN, J. P. A. οἰκεῖος, ἑταῖρος, ἐπιτήδειος, φίλος. Diss. Groningen, 1932.

FIELD, G. C. *Plato and his contemporaries*. Methuen, 1930.
FORBES, C. A. NEOI. Pub. Amer. Philolog. Ass., 1933.

GEFFCKEN, J. 'Das Rätsel des Kleitophon.' *Hermes*, LXVIII, 1933, 4.
GLOTZ, G. *La solidarité de la famille dans le droit ancien*. Paris, 1905.
GRUBE, G. M. A. *Plato's Thought*. Methuen, 1935.

KRAMER, H. *Quid valeat ὁμόνοια in litteris Graecis*. Diss. Göttingen, 1915.

LAGERBORG, R. *Platonische Liebe*. Leipzig, 1926.
LUTOSLAWSKI, W. *The origin and growth of Plato's Logic*. Longmans, 1917.

POHLENZ, M. *Aus Platos Werdezeit*. Berlin, 1913.
POLAND, F. *Geschichte des Griechischen Vereinswesens*. Leipzig, 1909.

RITTER, C. *Platon*. Berlin, 1931.
ROBIN, L. *La théorie platonicienne de l'amour*. Paris, 1908; 2nd edition, 1933.

Tod, M. N. In *Archives of the British School at Athens*, vol. xiii, pp. 328–338.

Walzer, R. *Magna Moralia und aristotelische Ethik.* (Neue Philologische Untersuchungen, vol. vii.) Berlin, 1929.
Wendland, P. *Anaximenes von Lampsacus.* Berlin, 1905.
Wilamowitz-Moellendorf, U. von. *Platon.* Berlin, 1919.

Ziebarth, E. *Das Griechische Vereinswesen.* (Preisschriften von der fürstlich Jablonowski'schen Gesellschaft, xxiv.) Leipzig, 1896.
— *Aus dem Griechischen Schulwesen.* Leipzig, 1909.

Aristotle, *Eudemian Ethics.*[1] Ed. Fritsche (1851), tr. J. Solomon (1915), tr. H. Rackham (1935).

Percival, Geoffrey. 'Notes on three passages from the *Nicomachean Ethics.*' *Classical Quarterly*, vol. xxix, July–October, 1935.

[1] Since the controversy is now concluded, I do not give references to those articles which discuss the relative dates of *E.E.* and *E.N.*

INTRODUCTION

Of the ten books of the *Nicomachean Ethics*, Aristotle devoted two to the discussion of friendship: and the attentive reader is at once inclined to ask the reason for so lengthy a treatment of this subject. Two reasons may be given. First, the concept of 'friendship' which he is discussing is a great deal wider than that which a modern reader would normally attach to the term: and second, Aristotle is dealing, even more than is his wont, both with problems which have been raised by other thinkers and with questions which arise out of his own observation of the daily life of his time. A short summary of the part played by friendship in Greek life, and of the treatment of friendship by other thinkers before Aristotle, will therefore be necessary for the full understanding of the material which he brings forward in Books VIII and IX of the *Nicomachean Ethics*.

Further, the method adopted in this edition is new: and it will therefore be necessary to state the reasons which have led me to adopt this method of exposition, and the difficulties which it is intended to meet. The second section of this introduction will deal with this topic.

I. FRIENDSHIP IN GREEK LIFE AND THOUGHT BEFORE ARISTOTLE

The term which Aristotle analyses in his treatment of friendship in the *Ethics* is an adjective.[1] This adjective

---

[1] φίλος.

may be active or passive in sense, and is usually translated 'friendly' or 'dear to' accordingly. When it is used as a noun, it is practically equivalent to the English 'friend', and the abstract noun[1] which is formed from it is accordingly equivalent to the English 'friendship'. The verb[2] which is formed from the same root means 'to treat as a friend', and may usually be rendered 'love' or 'like'. An analysis of the objects and persons to whom these terms are applied throws light on the part played by friendship in Greek life.

Our knowledge of Greek life may be said to begin with Homer, and the Heroic Age which he describes: and, in fact, the concept of friendship, which a Greek of the fourth century took for granted as a normal part of his life, was largely dominated by ideas which he had inherited from the Heroic Age. When Homer makes Odysseus speak not only of his 'dear wife', but also of his 'dear heart' and his 'dear hands', it is clear that this is not merely a freak of language. Philologists are agreed that the adjective is in origin possessive: and its application to objects as well as persons must indicate a regard that is possessive rather than affectionate in origin.

This is confirmed by the use of the noun: a Homeric Greek meant by his 'friends' all those upon whose assistance he could rely—all those who, in the English phrase, were 'his men'. Now the Homeric society was

---

[1] φιλία does not appear until the fifth century, and occurs mainly in prose writings. The earlier term is φιλότης, which never dies out of the usage of verse writers, and in later works is mainly applied to sexual love.
[2] φιλέω.

organized in groups, whose individual members were
bound to the support of one another and of the group.
In the days when piracy was an honourable profession,
and every stranger was therefore a potential enemy, it
was essential that a man should know upon whom he
could rely. The Homeric society is indeed beginning
to emerge from the primitive state of organization, in
which the family or the clan stands as the only group
to which the individual owes allegiance: but in its
practice of friendship it reflects clearly the practices of
that state.

Thus friendship in the Heroic Age denotes primarily
the solidarity which exists between the members of the
family: and the 'comrades'[1] who form the other class
of friends are bound to one another in a group whose
solidarity is similar to that of the family. The essence of
friendship lies in the duties of mutual support and
assistance which it imposes. The 'comrades' of war or
adventure in the Heroic Age are bound to aid, succour
or avenge one another: and the tie which binds them
to these duties is exactly analogous to the tie of blood
which binds the members of the family to the same
duties.

There is a danger that in dealing with the Heroic
Age we may be misled by the splendid example of
Achilles and Patroclus into supposing that friendship
would in every case be accompanied by an emotional
attachment as strong as that which existed between
these two. The truth is, rather, that Achilles in all that

[1] ἑταῖροι.

he does for Patroclus is merely carrying out the duties which were due to his comrade: and the intense emotional feeling, which leads Achilles into excesses, is extraneous to the normal idea of friendship between two comrades. Theseus and Pirithous, who formed their celebrated friendship by agreement after Pirithous had been caught in the act of stealing Theseus' cattle, and who seem simply to have joined together for their various enterprises, are a far better example of the ideal friendship of the Heroic Age: once their agreement is formed, they are loyal to the uttermost, but the beginning of their alliance at all events was due not to personal affection but to an overt agreement. Affection, in fact, may exist between friends in the Heroic Age, and sometimes does; but it is no essential part of friendship. The essence of friendship is its duties.

This 'group-concept', if we may so call it, is clearly to be seen in one institution of Greek life, which persists unchanged from the Heroic Age throughout the classical period: this is the institution of 'guest-friendship',[1] by which the guest, having come under the protection of the sacred hearth, and been assimilated to the family through the partaking of a meal, is bound to his host for the remainder of their respective lives. This bond is mutual: from thenceforth, each is bound to render hospitality to the other whenever it is required. In an age in which travelling was highly dangerous, the utility of this institution is obvious: it is a constant feature of Greek life. The guest-friends transmitted the

[1] ξενία.

bond in many cases to their descendants: who could renew the guest-friendship simply by meeting and acknowledging one another's claims. So Glaucus and Diomede, meeting on the field of battle, renew the pact of hospitality which has existed between their houses. Further, in later times at any rate, the friends of one of a pair of guest-friends could rely on the hospitality of the other: and so the wealthy Crito, in the Platonic dialogue which bears his name, can offer Socrates shelter and hospitality with his guest-friends in Thessaly. The 'hereditary guest-friend'[1] occupies an especially honoured position among the friends of a fourth- or fifth-century Greek: and while it does not seem that the analogy between the tie of guest-friend-ship and the tie of blood was consciously recognized by the Greeks themselves in later times, it is clear that in its origin the tie actually consisted in the creation of a factitious blood-relationship between host and guest.

A similar conception is to be seen in the ceremony of reconciliation: it would appear that in origin this ceremony, like the meal of guest-friendship, resulted in the admission of the former combatants into the same family. The underlying idea is clearly that the former enemy can only become a friend by being ad-mitted into the group of his friend-to-be. Normally, however, the reconciliation has only its minimum strength: and, though Homer speaks of it as 'friend-ship', it means to him no more than an agreement

[1] ξένος πατρικός (πατρῷος).

between the parties that each will refrain in the future from encroaching upon the other's rights. Homer can speak of the relationship existing between Odysseus and the relatives of the dead suitors, when Zeus has decreed that they be reconciled, as 'friendship'.

But this is really a peculiarity of the Heroic Age, at least in so far as it concerns the relations between individuals: although classical Greece does use very similar language of the relations of states. The Greek of the classical age does not put into practice the ideas of the Heroic Age without some modifications, due to changed conditions of society, and this is true of the Heroic Age idea of friendship. The broad outlines, however, can be recognized: in particular, the relationship of blood never ceases to lie at the centre of the theory and practice of friendship in Greek life.

If we compare the conditions of the fourth or fifth century with those of the Heroic Age, one difference stands out immediately. Friendship between persons who are not related by blood no longer implies the common membership of a group: it is determined by personal choice. 'Comradeship', in fact, has come to mean something far closer to personal friendship in the sense in which we know it. This does not mean that the group-concept has disappeared from Greek life: apart from the tie of blood, the Greeks never lose their feeling that the tie which unites the members of any group is friendship. It must be remembered in this connection that the Greek city included in itself a number of groups, ranging from the ancient clan divisions, which in Attica in classical times had only a religious significance, to purely social clubs.[1] It is the standing assumption of Greek political thought that the tie which unites the members of any state is friendship: and inscriptions (dating, it is true, mainly from the second and third centuries B.C.) not only testify to the number and variety of the clubs which existed both at Athens and throughout the whole of Greece, but also in a surprising number of cases expressly claim for the members the title of 'friends'.

But alongside the 'group-concept', there has also grown up the idea of a close personal friendship, based on a mutual esteem and affection. It is a fascinating study to watch the growth of this idea in the literature that has come down to us. In the lyrists of the seventh and sixth centuries, the tie of friendship is, on the one hand, based on personal companionship, and, on the other, it is dominated by the strict conception of duty which we saw in the Heroic Age. Archilochus calls down a curse upon the man who 'has wronged him, and has trampled on his pledges, though he was a former comrade': and it is an attractive assumption that the 'pledges' are the same thing as the 'mighty oath—the salt and the table', which his defaulting father-in-law-to-be, Lycambes, broke. Sappho, too, shows that 'comradeship' was coming to mean something close to personal friendship, as we know it: she

[1] The restored democracy at Athens prohibited the formation of political clubs: it appears that it was in these ἑταιρεῖαι that the oligarchical movements, which occurred toward the close of the Peloponnesian War, were organized.

can say that 'Leto and Niobe were very dear comrades'. Sappho further affords the sole instance of
which I know in Greek literature, of a lady consoling
a rejected suitor with the words 'But be my friend. . .'.
Such freedom of choice was not allowed to the women
of the mainland in classical times.

When we come to the Megarian Theognis, however,
the 'salt and the table' are no longer a 'mighty oath',
and he can warn his young friend that 'many men are
comrades in food and drink, but in serious action are
of poorer stuff'. Theognis, together with Hesiod, the
moralist of the Heroic Age, is important because his
utilitarian counsels, while they also reflect the spirit
and the particular conditions of his own days, were
used as a text-book for the education of children
throughout Greece of the classical period. Hesiod is
'legal' in his outlook on friendship: and Theognis,
while he no longer regards the wrath of the gods as
guaranteeing the bond of friendship, insists time and
again upon the necessity of loyalty to one's friends.
Both regard friendship as a means to the protection of
one's interests.

Utilitarianism, in fact, is the key-note of most of the
popular thought and practice of friendship in fifth-
century Greece. Friendship has become a matter of
personal alliance: but it is still an alliance made with
a view to furthering the interests of the parties. This
utilitarianism becomes explicit when friendship, in
common with the other moral ideas of the Greeks, is
subjected to systematic criticism by the sophists of the

fifth century. We also find that the familiar distinction of 'nature' and 'convention', which was applied by the sophists to the other moral ideas of Greece, was applied to friendship as well: in general, it is accepted that it is the tie of blood which exists 'by nature', other forms of friendship existing 'by convention'.

But the enquiry into ethical ideas was carried further than this point, to the attempt to find some fundamental explanation of the attraction of one individual for another. Two views are put forward: that friendship is based on likeness, and that it is based on opposition. These views appear not only in the ethical thought of the fifth century, but in the physical speculations of the pre-Socratic philosophers. When we meet them first in the teaching of Anaximander, it is clear that they are not used with any conscious ethical bearing: his assumption that like is drawn to like is conceived as a natural law of the physical universe, and his doctrine of the warfare of the unlike elements, though ultimately it is drawn from the notion of sexual opposition and union, is not put forward with any conscious reference to human conduct. Heraclitus, again, who maintained that it was the balanced opposition of opposed elements which produced the harmony of the universe, drew on the analogy of sexual love: but his fragments do not lead one to suppose that he applied his principle of 'union in opposition' as an ethical speculation with direct reference to human affairs. Empedocles, however, though he still assumes as a law of nature that like things are attracted to like, did apply his physical theories in some sense to human conduct. The parallelism between the two parts of his work may not be exact in every detail: but it is clear that the 'Reign of Love' in his physical scheme, when the unlike elements are mingled together, is meant to correspond to the 'Reign of Aphrodite' in the Purifications—a golden age of peace in which there was no hostility between man and beast.

This aspect of Empedocles' work may be due to the influence of the Pythagoreans of Magna Graecia, with whom he is known to have been in contact. The Pythagoreans, indeed, attached great importance to friendship. In contrast to the physical philosophers of Ionia, Pythagoras attempted to establish a correspondence between his physical and his ethical teaching. We have not a great deal of trustworthy information concerning early Pythagoreanism: but the influence of the school upon Plato, and through him upon Aristotle, makes what we do know of high importance. The school seems to have been organized as a close corporation, between whose members 'friendship' existed as a matter of course: and the proverbs 'friends share their goods' and 'friendship is equality'—both of which are ascribed to the invention of Pythagoras—seem to have been used as a justification of some form of communism within the order. I believe that the interpretation of the second proverb varied during the history of the school; and that the 'arithmetical' equality of the early period gave place to a 'geometrical' equality, which justified the existence of grades within the order by the appeal to proportion as an essential principle of the universe.

In any event, the ideas of the philosophers are taken from their purely physical context, and applied to the problems of human conduct. So we find that Hippias, in Plato's *Protagoras*, represents that the present company, since they are alike, are bound together by the strongest ties of friendship: he does not, however, make clear wherein their 'likeness' consists, nor does he develop his theme. Generally speaking, the sophists do not develop popular thought to its logical conclusions, but they do present it in a systematic form. They do not relate it to a reasoned valuation of human life: and Plato's objection to their teaching is precisely this: that if it is developed to its logical conclusions it leads straight to anarchy.

Socrates, on the other hand, if we are to believe the evidence of Xenophon, was thorough-going in his utilitarianism. But the man in the street, in Greece as elsewhere, was given to a rather muddled form of 'noble inconsistency': and therefore the memory of Socrates could be attacked by the sophist Polycrates, on the ground that he threw scorn on the ties of family and friendship. Xenophon's defence is easy: Socrates did teach that one should not rely on the tie of blood alone, but he also taught that one should merit the attachment of one's kinsfolk and friends by the services which one renders to them. It would appear that Socrates regarded both blood relationship and the friendship of persons otherwise unrelated as simple alliances of mutual service, differing only in the fact that we choose our personal friends, whereas our parents confer the benefit of birth and nurture upon us without any action on our part. Both alliances are called into being by the doing of services, and exist for the mutual benefit of the parties concerned. The fragments of Democritus show a somewhat similar utilitarianism.

Socrates was remarkable in democratic Athens for his connection with the philo-Laconian aristocrats: and he appears to have held a doctrine of love[1] which was parallel to, if not founded upon, the Spartan view of homosexual love. In Sparta, and likewise in Dorian Crete, homosexual love was a public institution: while the actual practices of paederasty were regarded with scorn and disapproval, it was believed that the love of a young man for a youth could have the most beneficial results. The 'beloved'[2] was to be filled with the manly qualities of his 'lover': and this form of friendship was regarded with public approval. Now in Athens, and apparently in most of the other non-Dorian states, homosexual love was condemned altogether: it was not believed that any good result could come of it. The difference between Athens and Sparta is simply that while in both cities the actual gratification of homosexual passion was condemned, at Sparta there existed the belief that the homosexual attachment could be spiritualized, and should issue in the development of the highest personal qualities.

---

[1] ἔρως.

[2] The Spartan terms mean 'listener' and 'inspirer' respectively.

Now Socrates, as is well known, distinguished sharply between the body and the soul, and believed the soul to be the more important part of us: in contrast to the common view of his day, he appears to have attributed to the soul most of the functions and attributes which we understand by the 'personality'. Thus he held that love could be directed not to the body but to the soul: and he appears to have regarded this 'love of the soul' in much the same light as the Spartans regarded their higher form of homosexual love. Unfortunately, we have no Socratic psychology which could support this doctrine: and it is better to accept the fact that Xenophon, if he knew of one, did not see fit to describe it, and to rest content with the knowledge that Socrates did believe in the possibility of a 'love of the soul'. For Socrates' belief reappears in a developed form in the dialogues of his younger friend, Plato.

The Platonic theory of love has attracted perhaps more attention than any other of the Platonic doctrines: but I believe that its importance is greater for the understanding of Plato's metaphysics than for the understanding of his ethics. Plato devoted only one dialogue, the *Lysis*, to friendship: and the *Lysis* has been somewhat neglected, while attention has been focused on the brilliant pictures of love given in the *Symposium* and the *Phaedrus*. The *Lysis* gives a sober analysis of attraction, as it occurs between two human beings: and passes from that to the consideration of the object of attraction in its most general terms. Two conclusions emerge from the dialogue. The first is that

friendship is possible only between the good: the base
are bound to quarrel. This is not metaphysics, but
practical ethics, a clear statement of what has been
current in Greek thought (sometimes explicitly stated,
sometimes not) since the days of Theognis: a good
moral character is necessary before friendship can be
satisfactory. The second conclusion, which belongs to
psychological theory, is that the cause of attraction is
desire: and that the object of this desire is something
that is good absolutely, not merely good as a means to
some further good. Further, desire is a sign of im-
perfection, since it implies need.

The *Symposium* makes clear what it is that forms the
object of desire: it is the eternal Form, the knowledge
of which the soul lost on her entry into the body, and
which she must regain if she is to regain her former
perfection. Beauty appears to occupy a special position
in the hierarchy of Forms, in that it is beauty, more than
any other quality, which awakens in man the desire
which is, as it were, the mainspring of his energy. This
desire should be turned away from the beloved person,
who is only one example of many beautiful things on
this earth, to the eternal Beauty itself: but man may,
of course, rest content with the beauty that is of this
world, and find a purely sensual satisfaction. The importance which Plato attaches to Love[1] is that it represents for him the source of energy which man needs if
he is to carry out his philosophic quest. The highest
form of friendship is that between two persons who are

---

[1] ἔρως.

united in the pursuit of virtue: and Plato condemns the love of the body, though he sympathizes to some extent with those persons who are neither completely sensual nor in full control of their bodily desires.

Plato seems to regard the highest form of friendship as occurring most frequently between an older and a younger man. He had constantly before his mind the example of Socrates; and, in his own experience, his friendship for Dion, the Sicilian to whom he owed his unsuccessful entry into the politics of Sicily, seems to have been of this type.

At the end of his life, Plato expresses in the *Laws* his considered verdict on friendship: and his doctrine is unaltered, although his practical provisions show an increase in austerity. The highest type of friendship is to be encouraged in the state, but the 'mixed' type, and the purely sensual type, are to be banned. Friendship also appears to have occupied the attention of his pupils during this time: and the pseudo-Platonic *Clitopho*, written probably very soon after his death, presents a doctrine of friendship which receives a good deal of attention from Aristotle in the *Eudemian Ethics*. This is the distinction between one true form of friendship, and others, such as the friendships of children and animals; these, because they are harmful in their effects, whereas true friendship is not, are not to be called friendships at all. Aristotle's triple division of friendship, based on his distinction of three objects of desire, enables him to deal satisfactorily with this doctrine: and his opponents in the logical quarrel seem to have given him best, for he does not mention the matter in the later *Nicomachean Ethics*.

The *Eudemian Ethics* need not be discussed here: for their essential teaching is reproduced in the developed treatment of the *Nicomachean Ethics*. It is clear in both treatises that Aristotle is assuming in his hearers some knowledge of Plato, and of the questions which he raised. It is noteworthy, however, that he does not mention, even implicitly, the Platonic doctrine of love. No doubt he felt it to be unnecessary: for since his abandonment of the belief in the transcendent Form as the foundation of reality, his rejection of the Platonic doctrine which was based on that belief follows automatically. To Aristotle, the highest type of friendship is still that between two good men: but the good which is the object of their friendship consists in their characters, and is immanent, not transcendent.

With one question raised by Plato, however, Aristotle must deal at some length. Plato had laid down that a perfect being will be sufficient to itself, and having no needs will therefore have no need of friendship: this doctrine Aristotle accepts. He has therefore to make clear in what sense he believes that friendship is necessary for the good life. This he can do by his doctrine of friendship as the extension of self-consciousness. This problem, which appears in the *Eudemian Ethics* with a clear reference to the Academy, is stated in the *Nicomachean Ethics* without any such reference. So also is the problem of self-love, which is handled in a manner that betrays its Platonic origin, but without any explicit reference to Plato. In the *Nicomachean Ethics*, Aristotle draws very fully upon previous thought, and upon contemporary life: but his tone is independent. He speaks as the master of his own school: and his teaching may be allowed to stand as the original construction of his accurate mind.

II. THE METHOD ADOPTED IN THIS EDITION

It may appear that a new edition of a part of the *Nicomachean Ethics* is to say the least unnecessary: and a glance at the bibliography contained in Apelt's Teubner edition certainly tends to confirm that impression. Moreover, since the appearance of the Oxford translation of Dr Ross and the Loeb edition of Mr Rackham, it would seem that enough has been done not only for classical scholars but also for those who read the *Nicomachean Ethics* for their intrinsic interest, and to whom the knowledge of the ancient world is of little or no consequence. I therefore feel that this edition, which I hope will appeal to both sets of readers, needs a special apology.

A careful reading of even one page of Aristotle's text, and the collation of the notes which have been published on that page, together with the translations, leaves the reader with a feeling not far from despair. He will have been introduced to the Aristotelian doctrines which underlie the thought of the passage: he will be able to turn the passage into elegant and forceful English: and he will know something of the bearing which the thought expressed in his passage has on the general structure of Aristotle's thought. But if he is to be satisfied that he has mastered the passage, he must still do some hard thinking. He must know not only what each word means, but why it has been introduced at that particular point: and to discover that, he has generally to rely upon the guidance of his own wits.

This difficulty seems to me to be peculiar to Aristotle among ancient writers: and I do not believe that it is possible, by a simple translation, to surmount it. Abrupt turns in the argument, and syllogisms of which only one premise is expressed, are as mystifying in English as they are in Greek. It may seem, therefore, that the course of the argument should be indicated by means of notes: and this is indeed possible. When I commenced work upon *E.N.* viii and ix, I intended to do this: and I constructed a full commentary upon the first seven chapters of Book viii. This commentary is still in my possession: its bulk makes it quite unreadable. There is hardly a line which does not call for explanation of some sort. The question which must constantly be answered is not only 'What does Aristotle say here?' but 'Why does he say this particular thing at this particular point?'

It seemed to me that Stewart was on the right lines, when he prefixed to his commentary upon each chapter a paraphrase of the chapter. But to Stewart's paraphrase there is one weighty objection: it is frequently almost impossible to see how the sense which he gives is to be extracted from Aristotle's Greek. This is inevitable, if the order of ideas is disturbed: it is frequently a simple matter to rearrange them in an apparently logical order, whereas to recognize that particular logical sequence, in the apparently random collection of Greek sentences before one, is far from simple.

The method of editing which is put forward in this book is intended to make clear not only what Aristotle says, but what he means. I have treated his text as though it were (as indeed I believe that it is) lecture-notes: and the full text of my 'expanded translation' represents the lecture as it should have been delivered. Thus the expanded translation as a whole can be read continuously: and the reader is able to grasp the meaning without diverting his attention to foot-notes. Further, the explanatory matter is distinguished from the translation by italics: and, if the italicized words be passed over in reading, it will be found that the words printed in Roman type can be read continuously, as a plain translation of the text. The reader is therefore able to grasp not only what Aristotle means, but also how much of his meaning he has left unsaid. I have tried to make clear every point of the argument, however small it may be.

This particular difficulty of the logical sequence of the argument seems to me, as I have said, to be peculiar to Aristotle among ancient writers: and I would not put forward this method of editing as suitable for Plato.[1] Professor Cornford has done what is necessary

[1] It might, perhaps, be applied to Cicero's philosophical works.

to guide future editors of Plato. In fact, it is barely possible, by my method, to add anything to Plato's meaning: the following is an attempt to treat a page of the *Phaedo* (106 b 1–107 a 1) as I have treated the *Ethics*.

'Is not this, then,' he said, 'necessarily the truth about what is deathless, *namely that like our other examples it retires intact when it comes into contact with something that is opposed to its essential quality? We have proved that it cannot be destroyed.* If what is deathless is also indestructible, it is not possible for soul, whenever death comes against it, to be destroyed: for it follows from our previous argument that it will not admit death or (*to put the matter more simply*) be dead, in just the same way as three, we agreed, will not be even, and what is odd, again, *will not be even,* nor will fire be cold, nor, indeed, will the heat that is in the fire *be cold. Our examples, however, might be misleading: and we must not regard them as offering an analogy at all points.* 'Why should it not be the case', someone might urge, 'that what is odd should not become even when what is even comes against it, as we have agreed *that it cannot become possessed of the quality of evenness which is opposed to it,* but that it should be destroyed, and something even have come into being in its place?' *As regards the particular example, this is a serious objection.* If a man did urge this, we could not maintain against him that what is odd is not destroyed: for what is uneven is not *of its own nature* indestructible, *so that it is certainly possible for it to be destroyed.* If we had agreed that it is indestructible,

*we could have disposed of the objection at once, for if it cannot
be destroyed there is only one other possibility:* we could
easily have maintained that when what is even comes
against them, what is odd and what is three take flight
and go away. *The same is true of all our examples:* we
should have maintained the same position in the case
of fire and what is hot and the rest, should we not?'

'Certainly we should,' *replied Cebes.*

'*Well,*' said Socrates, '*this is really what we want to
prove about the soul: it cannot exist in a dead condition; but
can we agree that it is indestructible, and does not simply
vanish?* In the case of what is deathless, then, if we are
agreed that it is also indestructible, the soul in addition
to being deathless will also be indestructible: if we are
not agreed on this, we must discuss the matter further.'

'There is no need of further argument on that score
at all events,' said *Cebes:* 'for you will hardly find anything that does not admit of destruction, if what is
deathless, which is also eternal, is to admit of destruction.'

'Yes, this is true of God, I imagine,' said Socrates,
'and of the Form of life, and the other things that are
deathless: everyone would agree that they are never
destroyed.'

'Everyone indeed,' said *Cebes,* 'both men and still
more certainly, I imagine, gods—*they would certainly
agree about themselves that they are both deathless and indestructible.*'

'Then *we may take it as proved in the case of the soul,
may we not?*' said Socrates. 'Since what is deathless is

also indestructible, must it not be that soul, if it really is deathless, must also be indestructible?'

'It certainly must,' *said Cebes.*

'Then *we have proved our case,' said Socrates: 'for what is deathless, since it is indestructible, cannot either be dead or be destroyed, and there is only the one other possibility.* When death comes against a man what is mortal in him, *namely his body,* apparently dies, *for there is no reason why it should not admit of death:* but what is deathless in him, *namely his soul,* is intact and indestructible, and it takes flight and goes away, since it retires before death, *and does not admit either death or destruction to itself.'*

'This seems to follow,' *said Cebes.*

'*That,* then, my dear Cebes,' said *Socrates,* '*is our conclusion:* it is certain and proved that soul is deathless and indestructible; and *this means that its life is everlasting, so that* in good truth our souls will exist in Hades.'

I do not feel that the difficulties of this passage are removed by the expansion; in fact, it has been made not more but less intelligible, as well as less readable. The interplay of conversation and thought retires on the approach of logical expansion, and what is left is the dull and lifeless body. Plato's thought is no easier to grasp because it has been logically expanded: for its difficulties lie not in the form into which the ideas are cast but in the ideas themselves. If these cannot be grasped from an accurate translation, there is little hope that they will be the more comprehensible for being expanded.

Aristotle, however, presents the reader with an entirely different set of problems. I give below my 'expanded translation' of a representative passage from the *Ethics* (VIII, 6, 1, 1158 a 1–10):

'*We spoke before of the occurrence of friendship between persons who did not indulge in friendly intercourse: and we can now see how this can be.* Among the sour-tempered, and those of an elderly habit of mind, friendship is found less often, and at a lower degree, precisely because, and in exact proportion as, they are worse-tempered—*i.e. less inclined to avoid giving pain to others*—and take less pleasure in social intercourse. For an easy temper—*the desire to avoid giving pain*—and the active pleasure taken in social intercourse seem (*as we saw*) to be the marks most characteristic of friends. *Now we know that the activities which proceed from a disposition are precisely the same as those which go to form the disposition:* it follows that "good temper and sociability" are the things which most tend to give rise to friendship, *for on them are based the activities of friendship. We know that the young live by the guidance of their emotions, seeking pleasure and shunning pain without reflection: and they do take pleasure in the company of others. The sour-tempered and elderly, on the other hand, do not.* This is why the young, *since they pursue the pleasure which other people can give,* form friendships—*or, more strictly, act as friends toward those who give them pleasure*—quickly, while the elderly, *who lack the incentive of pleasure and are prone to caution,* do not *form friendships quickly, but take a long time to form connections.* Men will not form friendships with persons whose company gives them no pleasure, *because the activity of friendship is based upon the pleasure taken in our friends' company: and the elderly do not give one another any pleasure.* (The same is true of those persons *of other ages* who are sour-tempered.) *Men of this type may approve of one another personally without deriving pleasure from one another's society: and so they may form a disposition to wish each other well, and render each other material services, without the disposition to seek one another's company. Where they form such a disposition,* we may say that they are "well-disposed" to each other, inasmuch as they wish one another well and rally to each other's assistance in case of need—*two of the marks of friendship*—but they can hardly be called "friends", because their disposition, *though directed towards each other personally and not incidentally, issues in an activity which* lacks the daily intercourse and pleasure in one another's company which, as we saw, are held to be the greatest marks of friendship. *Their disposition falls short of the disposition of friendship in precisely the same respect as their liking for each other falls short of the liking which true friends feel for each other.'*

This passage represents ten lines of the Greek text: and if the explanatory matter is removed the translation reads as follows:

'Among the sour-tempered, and those of an elderly habit of mind, friendship is found less often, and at a lower degree, precisely because, and in exact proportion as, they are worse-tempered and take less pleasure in social intercourse. For an easy temper and the active pleasure taken in social intercourse seem to be the marks most characteristic of friends: it follows that "good temper and sociability" are the things which most tend to give rise to friendship. This is why the young form friendships quickly, while the elderly do not. Men will not form friendships with persons whose company gives them no pleasure. (The same is true of those persons who are sour-tempered.) We may say that they are "well-disposed" to each other, inasmuch as they wish one another well and rally to each other's assistance in case of need, but they can hardly be called "friends", because their disposition lacks the daily intercourse and pleasure in one another's company which, as we saw, are held to be the greatest marks of friendship.'

This translation does, I think, give an adequate representation of what Aristotle actually says. It has, of course, been influenced in wording by the view which I take of the passage as a whole: but that is inevitable, and I must confess that to construct an expanded translation, of which the translation proper shall read continuously without admitting some roughnesses of style, has proved a task beyond my capacity. It is a brief passage, and I do not think that it is unfairly chosen: for while it certainly does provide typical examples of the problems which are indigenous to Aristotle's text, these are no more numerous, and no more obscure, than those of other passages which might have been chosen. The following points may seem to call for explanation:

Aristotle has given no indication of the bearing which the passage has upon the argument of the book as a whole. He simply brings forward his facts, and the reader must fit them together as best he may. It is clear that the same facts may be used for different purposes: and until the reader has assured himself as to the purpose for which Aristotle is using his facts, he cannot feel certain of the interpretation of the facts at any given point.

Further, the words 'it follows that' in my translation represent an 'and' in the original Greek. When Aristotle connects two words (or two clauses) by 'and' he may mean one of three things: the second word may simply be added to the first, as a second point for consideration: it may be a more accurate definition of the subject, which he means to substitute for the first word: or it may be an inference from the first word. In the first case, 'and' is generally an adequate rendering: in the second, 'i.e., that is to say', gives the sense: and in the third, 'and therefore' is usually correct. In both the last two cases, it may be necessary, if the full sense is to be grasped, to give the concealed argument which justifies the substitution or the inference. It seems clear to me that the present case is an inference: I have therefore supplied the intermediate step in the argument, and punctuated my expansion as seemed most convenient.

I make no apology for what may seem to some to be an excessive wordiness in my expansion. Throughout the two books of this edition, my aim has been to make clear every point in the argument which I felt to be in the least degree obscure: I have therefore attempted above all to make the sense clear, even at the cost of conciseness.

The text used is that of Burnet, which differs very slightly from the Oxford text of Bywater. I note any radical departures from the Oxford text: and it is intended that the 'expanded translation' may be read concurrently with the Oxford text. In many cases, the view taken of the sense will be seen to involve a different punctuation of the text: but I do not feel that this difficulty is such as to justify the appearance of a new text.

Scholars may find it a grave defect in this method that they will find in my expansion only the view which I myself take of the text at any particular point, without any statement of the reasoning which has led me to adopt this view, or discussion of the views of others from whom I differ. I acknowledge freely that my view may be, and in many cases probably is, liable to correction: and I feel also that it is a defect in my method that it prevents me from acknowledging my debt to others whose view of the text is adopted. In any event, I would accept full responsibility for the view taken of the text at any point. Against these objections, I feel that this method of editing has enabled me to raise all, not merely some, of the points in which Aristotle's text calls for explanation. For this reason, I would put forward this method of editing for the consideration of scholars, in the hope that it may lead to what I believe to be the first need of Aristotelian scholarship—the thorough examination and exposition of the detailed problems of the Greek text.

ARISTOTLE ON FRIENDSHIP

THE NICOMACHEAN ETHICS

Book VIII

I

Our next business after this will be to discuss friendship. *We can give several good reasons why friendship should be included in our course on ethics: they fall under two main heads.*

(*a*) Friendship is a virtue, *as we saw in our discussion of the virtues of social life: or if this statement appears strange to those among us who do not usually understand by friendship a characteristic of an individual, we may perhaps say that it involves virtue, as it is a relation which can only exist between good people. In either case, to say so much implies that friendship is a noble thing—i.e. that it is worthy to be pursued as an end in itself.*

(*b*) Further, friendship is among the most indispensable requirements of life: *it is, in fact, valuable not only as an end, but as a necessary means to life.*

If we can produce facts to support these contentions, it will readily be seen that we shall do well to discuss friendship. We will take first those considerations which fall under (b): these again may conveniently be ranged in three divisions.

PA

I

(i) *It is an observed fact that men find friendship indispensable in good fortune, in bad fortune, and at all periods of their life.*

In good fortune:—No one, *if he were allowed to choose,* would choose to live without friends, but in possession of all the other goods. In fact, it is *commonly* held that rich men, rulers, and potentates, *who are commonly regarded as having the good things of life,* need friends more than anyone else—*for two reasons.* What, *men urge,* is the use of such prosperity, if you take away the opportunity of beneficence, which is most commonly displayed towards friends, and meets with the greatest praise when displayed towards friends? *Without friends, they can neither practise their goodness, nor obtain recognition for it.* Or again, how can their prosperity be safeguarded and preserved, without friends? The greater it is, the more it is exposed to dangers—*and the greater is the need of friends who will protect it.*

In bad fortune:—In poverty, or any other misfortune, men think that their friends are their only resource.

And at all ages:—Friendship is an aid to the young, enabling them *through the advice of those who are more experienced in life* to avoid error; to the elderly, supplying them with service and supplementing their failing powers of action; and to those in their prime, assisting them to perform noble deeds—*as the saying of Diomede has it,* 'when twain together go', they are better able not only, *as Plato reminds us,* to think, but also to act.

(ii) Again, *friendship is natural, so that it must be a means to the good for man which nature strives to realize: we will cite the two most commonly observed instances of natural friendship.* (α) Friendship seems to exist naturally both in parent for offspring and in offspring for parent (this fact, *which is commonly recognized,* holds true not only in the case of man but in the case of birds and the majority of animals as well). And (β) friendship seems to exist naturally between members of the same species: this is especially true in the case of mankind, and this is the reason why *in the case of mankind we actually have a special word 'kindliness'*[1] *to designate this natural friendship—and* 'kindly' is *in fact* used as a term of praise. As further evidence *of the existence of this form of natural friendship we may add the evidence of observation to that of language.* We may see when on our travels how man belongs, *as it were,* to man, i.e. is a friend to him.

(iii) Again, it appears that it is friendship which holds cities together *by forming the bond between their members. It will follow that friendship merits discussion as a necessary means to the realization of the end for man, no less than justice, which ensures right conduct between the citizens: in fact, we can see at once that there must be some close connection between friendship and justice. Three considerations will illustrate this point.* (α) It appears that *this is why* lawgivers, *whose opinions are unfettered by ulterior motives, and whose choice is therefore highly significant, are seen to* set more store by friendship than they do by justice. *The facts are these:—*Concord, *which everyone knows to be essential to the maintenance of a constitution,* appears to be akin to friendship, and they aim at securing concord before

---

[1] φιλανθρωπία: the quality of 'loving men'. There is no term φίλιππος to designate the love of horses for horses: but there is a term by which we designate the love of men for men.

anything else, and at banishing *its opposite*, faction, before anything else. (Now faction is *clearly a form of* enmity, *which is the opposite of friendship: and this goes some way to prove our assertion of the relationship of friendship and concord.*) (β) Further, when men are friends, there is no need of justice *to make them refrain from injuring one another:* but even though they are just, they still need friendship *to make them come together in the first place.* (γ) Again, *acts of equity, which are* the highest form of just actions, seem *to most people* to contain an element of friendship.

So much for the considerations falling under (b). Let us see what reasons appear for regarding friendship as an end in itself. (*a*) Friendship is not only necessary as a means: it is also a noble thing—*nobility being the consummation of virtue. Three opinions, each of which is accepted at least by some persons, may be cited in support of this statement.*

(i) We *commonly* praise those who love their friends, *as though their action proceeded from a virtue.*

(ii) Also, the possession of many friends is *commonly* thought to be a noble thing.

(iii) Again, some people[1]—*we may call to mind the arguments of Plato's 'Lysis'*—think that it is the same people who are good men and friends: *this view would appear to make friendship and virtue co-extensive, and clearly implies that friendship is a noble thing.*

We can give good reasons, then, for including friendship in our course on ethics: and we shall not be the first to discuss friendship. In fact, it has been much discussed in the past:

---

[1] ἔνιοι.

popular proverbs and the sayings of great men alike bear witness to the interest which it has aroused. We will cite a few of these: they will serve to show the lines along which previous thought on friendship has run, and so make clear to us some of the problems which we have to face.

More than a few matters concerning its nature are subjects of debate. *Two main propositions are put forward.* Some people define friendship as a kind of likeness, in the sense that like people are friends—hence come the proverbs '*God ever leads* like to like', 'Jackdaw to jackdaw', and so on. Others take the opposite view: they *use Hesiod's phrase, and* say that men who are alike are always 'potters' to one another. And on these very questions *of whether likeness or unlikeness forms the ground of attraction*, men search for an explanation that goes higher up *in the series of causes*, i.e. one that is grounded rather in the nature of the physical universe *than in the nature of man alone.* Euripides, for instance, *presupposing that it is desire which unites opposites in the realm of physics*, says that 'Earth yearneth for the rain' when dried up, 'And the majestic Heaven when filled with rain yearneth to fall to earth': and Heraclitus says that 'Opposition unites', and 'Discordant elements make the fairest harmony', and 'All things come to be through strife'. The opposite view finds its supporters, notable among whom is Empedocles, who maintains that 'Like seeks after like'—*assuming this, in fact, as though it were an ultimate principle, while to effect the junction of opposites an external force, 'Love', is necessary.*

Now these physical problems may be dismissed at

once, for they are foreign to our present enquiry: *they belong to physics, and could only be discussed in the light of the subject-matter of physics.* Let us examine those problems which relate to human life, and involve the character and emotions *of men: these are the subject-matter proper to ethics.* Let us see, for instance, whether friendship can arise in all men without distinction, or whether it is true, *as the arguments of the 'Lysis' seem to show—the view, indeed, has frequently been put forward*—that bad men cannot be friends. Another problem which we must face is whether there is one species of friendship or several. *The solution which has been propounded by our Academic friends need not be binding on us.* Those who hold that there is only one species, on the ground that friendship admits of degree (*for one can admittedly be more or less friendly or dear to anyone*), have put their trust in an insufficient proof. *It is true that difference in degree cannot in itself constitute specific difference: but this does not mean, as they have taken it to mean, that it excludes specific difference,* for things which differ specifically do in fact admit of difference in degree. *Their argument, then, is not logically cogent: and the question remains open for discussion.*[1]

[1] Om. εἴρηται...ἔμπροσθεν. The reference cannot be found elsewhere in the Ethics: and the remark may possibly be an insertion on the part of some person who noted that there was certainly no discussion of this question of 'difference in degree' in what follows.

II

Perhaps the truth about these problems *which relate to human life* will become clear if we ascertain the nature of *whatever it is that forms the object of attraction*—'the lovable'.[1] *We shall, in fact, use the method 'examination of inflected forms', familiar to us from our logical studies: if the inflected form 'lovable' is found to be used in different senses with reference to different objects, it will follow that 'to love' and 'friendship' have these same differences.*

It is held (*we can use here without further enquiry the results of our previous examinations of the end of human action*) that it is not everything that is loved, but only that which is lovable: and that this is what is[2] either good, or pleasant, or useful. But it would seem that 'useful' means 'that by which we obtain some good or pleasure': so that the things lovable as ends will be the good and the pleasant.

But this bald statement might be misleading. In view of the difficulties in which previous thinkers have become involved, owing to their mistaken ideas on the good, we shall do well to remind ourselves of the distinctions which our previous examinations of this subject have brought to light. We need do no more than simply resume the argument: it is familiar to us all.

Do men, then, feel attraction toward (=desire, love) the Good (*i.e. what is good absolutely*) or what is good for

---

[1] τὸ φιλητόν. The word is a verbal adjective formed from the verb φιλέω.　　　　[2] ⟨τὸ⟩ Richards.

them? These sometimes clash: and this is true also of the pleasant—*that which is absolutely and in itself pleasant may not be pleasant to a particular person.* (*It will be observed that in our present discussion the substitution of 'pleasant' for 'good' would not injure our argument.*) It seems, then,[1] that every man loves what is good for him: that is to say, that while without qualification the good is lovable, relatively to any particular person that which is good for him is lovable to him. But in fact, *as we all know,* each man loves not what is really good for him, but what appears to him to be good for him. *Whereas in the case of a good man, that which is good absolutely is not only good for him, but appears to him to be so, the rest of mankind merely love what appears to them to be good for them; which may or may not be so, and which furthermore may or may not be absolutely good.* But this distinction *of the real and apparent good* will make no difference to our argument: we shall understand by 'lovable' 'that which appears to be so to the person in question'.

To resume:—There are, then, three grounds on which men 'love': *the good, the useful, and the pleasant. But though we can infer at once from this that there will be three different kinds of affection,*[2] *the affection is not in itself sufficient to constitute friendship: we may now proceed further to establish the nature of friendship by examining certain marks which are assumed in the speech of everyday life as characteristic of friendship.*

Now the affection felt for inanimate objects is not called friendship: *and as our study is confined to human*

---

[1] δὴ Bywater, Rm.   [2] φίλησις.

friendship, it may be dismissed at once from our argument. We may, however, deduce from the negative fact the characteristics which are considered necessary, in addition to affection, for friendship. The characteristics which it lacks are three in number.

(*a*) There is not in it any reciprocation of affection, nor

(*b*) any wishing of good to the object. *People are certainly called 'lovers of wine', but* perhaps we may say that it would be absurd to wish wine well—if a man does it at all, he wishes the wine to keep well, so that he can have it himself. *We can see that his well-wishing is really directed not to the wine, but to himself:* whereas men say that we should wish well to a friend for the friend's sake, *and this disinterestedness is constantly assumed as a criterion of true friendship.* Now those who wish well to others in this way are *merely* called well-disposed,[1] if the other does not return the well-wishing, 'reciprocal goodwill' being the definition of friendship *which we may therefore assume that those who use this language would accept. Ought we to accept this as a complete definition,* or should we add *the characteristic*

(*c*) 'Known to both parties'? *'Reciprocal goodwill' does not seem to cover all the facts:* many people are well-disposed to persons whom they have never seen, but whom they believe to be good or useful: and one of these might well have the same feelings toward the first man. Here, then, we have people who are well-disposed to one another: but we could hardly call them

---

[1] εὖνοι.

friends, since they are not aware of their mutual regard. *Our definition of friendship, rough as it may be, must exclude such cases as this; so we will complete it by the stipulation that both parties must be aware of one another's feelings.*

We therefore *conclude that in order to be friends* men must be well-disposed to one another—that is, they must (*a*) (*b*) wish one another well: they must (*c*) both be aware of this: and the motive of their well-wishing must be one of those mentioned above *as constituting the possible grounds of affection.*

These things, however—*the good, the useful, and the pleasant*—differ from one another specifically: it follows that the affections *to which each of them gives rise* also differ specifically; and that the friendships *made up of these affections* differ specifically as well. *We can now answer the question asked in the previous chapter concerning the species of friendship.*

There are, therefore, three species of friendship, corresponding in number to the 'lovables'. *It is the difference of the 'lovable' which provides us with the specific differences which distinguish them: the three distinguishing marks which together make up our definition of friendship are present in each species.* Answering to each lovable there is (*a*) reciprocal affection which (*c*) is known to both parties: while those who love one another, inasmuch as they do love one another, (*b*) wish one another well.

III

We may now proceed to examine these three species or types of friendship, and see how they are related to each other. We have pointed out that the three marks of friendship are present in each: but we shall find that the differences between them are not precisely similar to those between species of the same genus, though for purposes of classification it has been convenient to treat them as such. We will take first the two 'lower' types, those based on utility and pleasure.

Those who base their affection on utility do not love one another 'in themselves'—*i.e. because of what each is in himself*—but inasmuch as each gets something good from the other. The same is true of those who base their affection on pleasure: *the ground of their affection is not the essential character of a man in himself, but the pleasure which they derive from him.* They do not, *for instance,* enjoy the society of witty persons in virtue of their essential quality as wits, but because they themselves find them pleasant.

Then—*to be more precise*—those who base their affection on utility love because of what is good for them, *not because of what is good absolutely,* and those who base their affection on pleasure love because of what is pleasant to them, *not because of what is pleasant absolutely:* that is to say, they love a man, not because he is lovable[1]—*i.e. good and pleasant absolutely*—but because he is useful or pleasant *relatively to them. Now the fact*

[1] οὐχ ᾗ <φιλητὸς> ὁ φιλούμενός ἐστιν.

that one man is useful or pleasant relatively to another is a logical accident of his being what he is: and so *we may say that* these friendships exist per accidens, since in them a man is loved not because he is the man he is, but because he provides some good or pleasure *which the other party happens to require at the moment.*

This 'accidental' quality explains why these two types of friendship are lacking in the permanence which is universally regarded as desirable in friendship. It follows that friendships of these types are easily dissolved, when the parties change: if they are no longer useful or pleasant *to one another, naturally* they cease to love *one another, and turn elsewhere in pursuit of their ends.*

This is especially true of the friendship that is based on utility, which we will now proceed to examine separately. Utility is not a permanent characteristic: different things are useful at different times, *so that people may very easily cease to find one another useful.* When, therefore, the ground of the friendship has ceased to exist, the friendship passes out of existence as well: for the friendship existed *simply* with reference to the goods which were to be realized through it. *We can see this happening every day in the world around us.*

Friendship of this type seems *in our experience* to occur most frequently between the elderly: people of advanced years *are naturally prone to it, as they generally* pursue profit and not pleasure. *But it is not confined to the elderly: it is the pursuit of profit which is its motive, and so* it also occurs commonly between those persons in their prime, and young persons, who pursue their own advantage *and not, as most persons of those ages do, honour or pleasure.*

We may note further that friendship of this type is lacking in one important characteristic which is possessed by each of the other two types. People of the nature described, *even though they are bound together in a friendship based on utility,* are not much given to constant daily inter-course, *such as is commonly accepted as characteristic of friends. Such intercourse depends for its existence upon the pleasure which we find in the companionship of our friends:* and people of this type do not even, in some cases, find one another pleasant at all. And so, *while in the other two types of friendship the daily intercourse is essential for the continuance of the friendship,* these people have no need of such intercourse with one another (unless it brings profit), *but can be friends without it. The pleasure which is contained in this type of friendship (for no type of friendship is wholly devoid of pleasure) is derived from the hope of profit: and so since* these persons find one another pleasant exactly in so far as they hope to obtain some good from one another, *they can often obtain that pleasure without having one another's society at all, and in any case will break off the friendship when the hope of profit is at an end.*

Among friendships of this type men *commonly* reckon the friendship of host and guest: *it is obviously under-taken simply for the mutual benefit of the parties, and it is quite independent of daily intercourse.*

These typical instances have illustrated sufficiently the nature of this type of friendship: we may now turn our atten-tion to the type that is based on pleasure. This is perhaps best

*illustrated by the friendship of the young, which is obviously
based as a rule on pleasure: of course, people of an undeveloped
and childish character exhibit the same characteristics.*

The friendship of the young seems to be based on
pleasure. They live by the guidance of their emotions,
*and not, as older persons tend to do, according to a reasoned
plan of life:* and *therefore, as the emotions are concerned
simply with pleasure and pain,* they generally pursue what
is pleasant to them—the pleasure, that is, of the
moment, *not the more distant pleasures which an elderly
person might pursue deliberately.* But as they advance in
years, *their tastes change rapidly, and accordingly* they find
different objects pleasant. Therefore, *since they make
friends to secure the particular pleasure of the moment,* they
make friends quickly and drop them quickly: for as
the pleasure in view changes, the friendship changes
also; and pleasure of this type, *which fulfils a momentary
desire,* is quick to change, *so that they must change their
friends quickly if they are to secure it.*

Another point *of interest concerning the young which may
be explained under this head* is that the young are given
to forming passionate attachments. *The explanation is
simple, in the light of what we have said:* the passionate
friendship depends largely upon emotion—it is based,
that is, on pleasure, *and that the pleasure of the moment.*
This is why the young, *even more than lovers proverbially
do,* fall in love quickly[1] and fall out of love as fast,
often changing their minds in the course of a single
day.

---

[1] φιλοῦσι ⟨τάχεως⟩ καὶ τάχεως παύονται Rm.

But *though the friendship that is based on pleasure is lacking in permanence,* the young (*we will keep to our example*) do wish to pass their days together, and to pass their lives in daily intercourse with their friends: by doing this, they obtain *the pleasure which is* the object of their friendship—*we have seen already that such intercourse depends on pleasure. This, then, is one mark popularly accepted as typical of friendship which the friendship that is based on pleasure possesses.*

These two types of friendship, then, fall short in various respects of the standard which is generally accepted: we may now turn to that type from which the common run of humanity derive their conceptions of what friendship should be. As is the rule in the case of things which, as friendship does, subsist by nature, where there are imperfect types we expect to find a perfect type.

Perfect friendship is that between men who are good, and *not only good but* alike in their virtue. *It contains in itself all the marks which we have seen to be characteristic of friendship.*

These persons wish one another well in like degree, *since they are alike in respect of the virtue for which each loves the other: so that the well-wishing is not only reciprocated but evenly reciprocated: and their well-wishing is entirely disinterested, since* they wish one another well because they are good, and, *virtue being an essential part of their character,* they are good in themselves, *not merely good relatively to a person who can obtain some further end through them.* Now those who wish their friends well for their friends' sakes (*as these people do*), *and not for the sake of their own advantage,* are most truly friends, *as we have already seen to be the popular opinion:* this is true, because *to wish one another well for their own sakes means that* the friendship exists because of each man's own self, and not accidentally *in virtue of the fact that the parties find one another pleasant or useful: each finds his motive in the other's essential character.*

It follows that *the perfect friendship possesses the permanence in which we found that the other two types were lacking.* The friendship of the good persists as long as they are good: and virtue is a lasting thing, *so the friendship, which lasts as long as its motive, must be permanent also.*

But besides possessing all the marks of friendship, the perfect friendship also, precisely because it is perfect, contains the advantages of the two less developed types. To take utility first:—Each of the two friends is good not only absolutely (*as ex hypothesi he must be*), but relatively to his friend: for good men are both good absolutely and, *since they improve one another by their association,* beneficial to one another. The case with regard to their pleasantness is the same. The good are pleasant both absolutely (*since what is absolutely good is absolutely pleasant*), and to one another: this is so, because everyone finds pleasure in his own actions, and *therefore* in actions of the same type as his own: and the actions of one good man are the same, or of the same type, as those of another, *so that each can find the other's actions pleasant.*

To sum up:—There is every reason why friendship of this type should be, *as we have already pointed out that it is,* lasting: in it there meet all the attributes which friends should have. All friendship is based upon good or pleasure: *which are* either absolutely *good and pleasant* (*that which is good absolutely being also pleasant absolutely*), or *good and pleasant* relatively to the friend, *as is the case in the two 'lower' types of friendship:* in which case the friendship is so called in virtue of a sort of resemblance, *whose nature we must explain later, which it bears to the perfect friendship.* In contrast *to these 'secondary' types of friendship, whose ground is, as already explained, a logical accident of the friends' natures,* all the advantages *of absolute and relative goodness and pleasantness* enumerated above inhere in the perfect friendship in virtue of the friends' own selves: they are alike both in their essential selves, *as being absolutely good, so that the absolute goodness and pleasantness certainly accrue to the friendship because of the friends' selves,* and in the other respects *enumerated, namely in goodness and pleasantness relatively to one another; as we proved a moment ago, it is their character, and not adventitious circumstances, which renders them both useful to one another by the mutual improvement which they attain, and pleasant to one another by their good actions.* Further, *the affection in this type of friendship, since it is directed to the man himself, because he is what he is, and not to him indirectly because he provides the ulterior object which his friend is seeking, is stronger than that in the other two types.* That which is good absolutely is also pleasant absolutely: now these are of all things the most lovable, *i.e. they arouse our affection more than anything else.* Between the good, therefore, *whose goodness and pleasantness are essential to their natures,* the affection (and *therefore* the friendship) is of the greatest intensity and of the most personal kind.

This, then, is the character of the perfect friendship: and if it occurs to us that we rarely see it in ordinary life, the reason is not far to seek. We might expect that friendships of this type should be rare: *its conditions are hard to satisfy.* Good men are few: and in addition, time and intimacy are necessary before it can come into existence, *and of course we have not unlimited time at our disposal in this short life. The friends must of course know one another's natures: and* as the saw has it, men cannot know one another until they have consumed the proverbial peck of salt together. No more, then, can they approve one another *without taking the time necessary to get to know one another,* or indeed be friends at all *in the true sense of the term,* before each sees that the other is worthy of affection ('lovable') and *therefore* feels *the* confidence in him *which one must feel in a friend.*

We often, of course, meet people who behave as though they were really and truly friends on a short acquaintance: but we know now that they cannot be friends in the true sense. Those who quickly exhibit toward one another the behaviour characteristic of friends, *certainly* wish to be friends: but *as we know,* they are not friends *in the true sense,* unless *besides liking one another* they are also lovable, and in addition know that they are. The wish to be friends is a quick growth: but friendship, *as we have seen,* is not.

IV

We are now in a position to clear up some of the questions which we raised concerning the nature of friendship: and in view of our discoveries as to the nature of the three types of friendship, we must examine more closely the relations which exist between them.

The conditions of the perfect friendship are as we have described them. This type of friendship, then, is perfect both in respect of the time *of its duration* and in respect of the other qualities *mentioned, namely absolute and relative goodness and pleasure:* and *an outstanding mark of its perfection is that* in respect of all these qualities each friend obtains the same satisfaction from the other—or *if it be objected that he cannot obtain exactly the same, then* a similar satisfaction; which *as all are agreed* should be the case between friends—*we can see that it will preserve the balance of the friendship by ensuring that each has the same reason for loving the other.*

It is this type which provides the norm by which we judge friendship: and the other two types resemble it in virtue of the fact that each possesses an element in common with it. The friendship that is based on pleasure bears a resemblance to it *in virtue of the element of pleasure which is common to them both,* since good men are in fact pleasant to one another: the same is true of that which is based upon utility, *the common element in this case being utility,* since good men are in fact useful to one another *in the way that we have seen.*

These two lower types also possess the characteristics of permanence and reciprocity, but in a less degree than the perfect type does. In the perfect type, they are both present to the fullest extent; in the two lower types, while we need not attempt to trace their interdependence, we may note that they appear to be present in a corresponding degree. Among these persons also friendship is most lasting when each friend obtains from the other the same thing, for instance pleasure—*we may discuss this case separately before considering utility.* The friendship is most lasting not only so, *when each friend obtains pleasure,* but when they obtain their pleasure from the same source, as do witty persons *who value one another for their wit,* not as a lover and his beloved.

These much discussed persons will explain our point well by providing an example of the contrary. They do not obtain their pleasure on the same terms: the lover obtains his by gazing upon the beloved, while the latter obtains his from the attentions paid to him by the lover; and as the beloved's beauty fades, the friendship sometimes fades too, *since neither has any longer the pleasure which provided its motive,* the lover no longer[1] finding the sight of his beloved pleasant, and the beloved *consequently* failing to obtain his attentions. On the other hand, *as is well known,* many lovers continue in friendship *even after the original pleasure is gone: but we must notice that in those cases the pleasure which is the motive of this kind of friendship has changed; it happens* if as a result of their intimacy they come to love one another's characters,

[1] οὐκέτι Rr.

their characters being of similar type *so that they can obtain pleasure from one another's actions. The baser sort of lovers need not detain us long: they do not even exchange different pleasures.* Those who exchange not pleasure for pleasure but pleasure for gain in matters of love are less closely friends and are also less permanent in their friendship *than those who exchange pleasures.*

The characteristic of permanence is even less marked in the friendship that is based on utility. Those who are friends for motives of utility part as soon as their profit ceases: they were friends not of one another, but of what they got out of one another, *and so can have no reason for continuing further in the friendship.*

As for the question which we asked at first, concerning the possibility of friendship between all types of men, the answer is simple in the light of what we have just established. A bad man cannot provide a good character as a motive for friendship: this much we may concede to those who have denied that bad men can enter into friendship at all. Pleasure and profit, however, do not depend on the character of the person who provides them. For motives of pleasure, then, and for motives of utility, bad men may be friends with one another, and good men may be friends with bad men, and one who is neither good nor bad may be friends with a man of any type of character at all: but for the motive of their own selves, it is obvious that none but the good can be friends, *since they alone possess a character that is lovable;* the bad, *since they are not lovable in themselves,* take no delight in one another, apart from the possibility of some advantage—*it may of course be either pleasure or profit.*

A further point *relating to the permanence of the perfect friendship* is that only the friendship of the good is proof against calumny. *It is obviously difficult to set at variance men who have satisfied the severe conditions of this type of friendship,* for it is not easy to believe anyone concerning what one has tested for oneself over a long period of time, *as the good friends have tested one another's character.* It is in them that we find the trust, and the feeling that 'he would never wrong me', and all the other things which people demand of true friendship.

The other types of friendship, however, are based on the accidental qualities of pleasure and utility, and not on the knowledge of the friends' characters: so that there is nothing to prevent the occurrence of suspicion and its kindred evils in the other friendships.

I call these types friendships, though it should be clear by now that the word is properly applied to the perfect friendship alone, these 'lower' types being rudimentary forms which do not deserve the name applied to the fully developed form: but provided we are not ourselves misled, there is no reason to depart from the usage of ordinary language. For since people call 'friends' both those who are bound together for motives of utility, as states *in the common parlance 'become friendly' (the instance is clear,* for the alliances between states are *commonly* recognized to be made for the sake of expediency), and those who base their affection for one another on pleasure, as children *'make friends', it may be as well if we use similar language.* Perhaps we too should call such people 'friends'; but *in that case, since we shall not be using the term in the same sense as we do in applying it to the perfect friends, we must* say that there are more species of friendship than one. *This, then, will be our answer to the question of whether there is one or more species of friendship: but we must be careful to understand what we mean by* '*species*' *here, for we do not mean species of one genus in the familiar sense.* That is to say, the friendship between good men which exists because they are good, *and not, as of course it might, because they are pleasant or useful to one another,* is friendship in the primary or proper sense, *since it alone shows friendship in its perfect or fully developed form.* The other friendships, *since they are more rudimentary,* are friendships in virtue of a resemblance *which they bear to the perfect friendship: they bear the same relation to the perfect friendship as the objects which provide their motive bear to the real good which is the motive of the perfect friendship.* In so far as the friends *in these unions* love something which is good *in their own eyes,* i.e. something which is similar *or analogous to the real good which the perfect friends love in one another's characters,* so far they are friends. What is pleasant is in fact good in the eyes of the pleasure-loving, *even as material profit is good in the eyes of the lovers of gain: and just as these objects are only good in a secondary sense, in virtue of the analogy which they bear to what is really good, so the friendships for which they provide the motive are friendships in a secondary sense, in virtue of the analogy which they bear to the perfect friendship whose motive is what is really good.*

But *we may note that* these friendships are not very apt to coincide—i.e. the same persons do not become friends for motives of pleasure and utility *at the same time:* the reason is, *in logical terms,* that accidental qualities, *such as utility and pleasantness with reference to a particular person,* are not often found in combination.

To sum up:—Friendship being divided into these species, the base will be friends for motives of pleasure or utility, since it is in this way, *by the accidental qualities of pleasantness or utility,* that they resemble one another *and therefore can supply one another's wants:* the good, on the other hand, will be friends for their own selves, since they are alike in so far as they are good, *and goodness is an essential quality of their characters.* They, then, are friends in the absolute sense, *as being lovable in themselves,* whereas the base are friends in virtue of an accident, *as they happen to find one another good or pleasant*— that is to say (*to put the matter in another way*), in virtue of the resemblance which they bear to the good friends *by being lovable in a secondary sense.*

So much, then, for the division of friendship into species: in order to obtain further light upon friendship, we must now examine the matter from another angle.

V

Beside the distinction made above of types of friendship, a distinction based on the object or motive of friendship, we may gain fresh knowledge of the nature of friendship by taking the parallel of the virtues, *and seeing how far this will lead us. We have seen that* when we call a man good, we mean either that he possesses a good disposition,[1] or that he is actually engaged in a good activity. The same distinction, *that of the disposition and the activity corresponding to it,* may be made in the case of friendship. When men take part in the daily intercourse of life together, they derive actual enjoyment from each other's company, and confer on each other the benefits *which we have seen to be a part of friendship.* On the other hand, when men who are friends are asleep, or are separated from one another by long distances, they do not manifest the activities of friendship: but *as they are friends,* they do possess the disposition to manifest these activities *toward each other. It 'is obvious, in fact, that* separation does not destroy friendship absolutely—*the disposition to act as a friend toward the person who is our friend*—while it does preclude the activities of friendship. (*We may note, however, that* there is a belief that lengthy separation does cause men to forget their friendship, *just as lack of practice destroys our capabilities in other respects:* this belief is embodied in the saying 'out of sight, out of mind'.) *The parallel of the virtues, then, has not been mis-*

---

[1] ἕξις.

leading: we can distinguish between the disposition and the activity of friendship.

Having established this distinction, it may be as well to go further, and examine the activity of friendship. We saw above that it is broken off by sleep or separation: but there may be other reasons why people do not practise it. *We may, then, gain a valuable insight into the nature of friendship, if we can establish any conclusion on this point. Now an obvious example of people who do form connections with one another, but do not spend their time in friendly intercourse together, is afforded by* the elderly, and those *of other ages* who are naturally of a sour temper. *They* seem, *on the face of it,* to have no capacity for friendship: *for they are not seen engaged in the activities proper to friends.* The reason is, that they have little in them that is pleasant: and no one can spend his days in friendly intercourse with one who is painful to him, or even not pleasant to him. It seems to be one of the strongest instincts of human nature to shun what is painful, and seek what is pleasant. People such as these approve of one another, *and therefore form connections:* but they do not spend their days in friendly intercourse.[1] *And where the activity occurring in a friendship is as restricted as it is here,* it seems more proper to call the parties 'well-disposed' than to call them 'friends'. For friendly intercourse is the activity which is most characteristic of friends. *We spoke of it above as though it were a mere means to the activities of conferring benefits and obtaining pleasure from the company of our friends. But we can see that it can con-*

[1] συμβίωσις, literally 'living together'.

stitute in itself the activity of friendship, and as such be sought as an end in itself. Material assistance is the chief aim of the needy, *and they tend to form friendships for the sake of obtaining this alone, without indulging in friendly intercourse further than is necessary to obtain it:* but even the supremely happy,[1] *who lack for nothing and so need not form friendships for the sake of material assistance,* seek daily companionship. In fact (*the reason need not detain us here*), they are the last persons to lead a solitary life. *Since, therefore, the supremely happy seek after the activity of friendly intercourse, and form friendships for that end alone, there is good reason for styling friendly intercourse the activity of friendship. Again, however, we see that the element of pleasure is essential to the activity: there are really two ways in which it enters into friendly intercourse.* Men cannot spend their time together in friendly intercourse unless they either (*a*) find each other pleasant in themselves—*in the strict sense of the terms, only the good can do this, for only they are of their own nature pleasant*—or (*b*) take pleasure in the same things—*as men of any type of character can do. We may note that* this *latter element* (*b*) seems certainly to be characteristic of comrades,[2] *who are an obvious example of friends who indulge in friendly intercourse.*

Now if the analogy of the virtues is to be trusted, we shall expect to find that the disposition of friendship arises from activities which are of the same character as those which issue from the disposition. We have analysed the object of friendship; and the result of this analysis should be of use in aiding

[1] μακάριοι: these are the persons who are fully supplied with this world's goods, and who therefore are free to spend their lives as they please.   [2] ἑταῖροι.

us to determine the character of the emotion[1] *which we expect to find in friendship, and consequently the character of the disposition which is formed from it.* Our analysis of the 'lovable' showed that, as we have often repeated, the friendship of the good is the most perfect form of friendship. *That this is true is shown by the nature of the affection contained in it, which is such as to form a specific disposition of friendship.* It is agreed that what is absolutely good or pleasant is the object of love and choice: while for any particular person, that which is good or pleasant relatively to him is the object of his love and choice. *Imperfect men do not 'love and choose' that which is absolutely good and pleasant, for it is not good and pleasant relatively to them:* but one good man is the object of love and choice to another good man for both reasons—*he is good and pleasant in himself, and he is also both good and pleasant relatively to the other. The affection of one good man for another, then, is directed toward the man himself: the reason for it resides in the character of the man, and is not something which can logically be separated from him, as are the relative good and pleasure which are the reasons why imperfect men are attracted to each other. Good men, then, 'like' each other in a peculiarly personal sense.*

'Liking',[2] however, seems to be an emotion, whereas friendship seems to be a disposition. *That means that through successive acts of liking, two good men arrive at a fixed disposition with regard to each other; and the fixed disposition to act in a friendly way to a given person is friendship. We can see that our distinction is valid from three considerations:*—

[1] πάθος.   [2] φίλησις.

First, liking is aroused in us *by any thing*, even by inanimate objects, *which we find good or pleasant, and therefore liking does not imply deliberate choice:*[1] whereas *friendship, as we saw earlier, implies reciprocation,* and the fact
that two men reciprocate each other's affection implies
that each exercises deliberate choice *in treating the other
(and not somebody else) as his friend. Now* deliberate
choice proceeds from a disposition, *and does not occur in
people unless they have such a disposition. The disposition
formed by imperfect people is a disposition to act as a friend
toward any person who can provide them with the good and
pleasure that they seek: and therefore they do not form a
specific disposition of friendship directed toward one person.
The good, on the other hand, as their disposition is formed
from an emotion which is really directed toward the men themselves, do form a disposition which may be described as a
'friendly disposition': each friend acquires the disposition to
treat the other, not any chance person, as a friend.*

Second, in the friendship of the good, the friends wish
well to each other for their own sakes. *As wish*[2] *is of
the end, not of the means, this implies that the friend is in
some sense (precisely in what sense will be explained later)
treated as an end. No emotion deals with anything apart
from the particular sensation which is its content:* so the friends
whose well-wishing is disinterested cannot be following
the guidance of their emotions, but must be acting in
accordance with a disposition—*for the apprehension of
an end requires a rational disposition of the desires.*

Third, we can see from the analysis of the lovable that the

[1] προαίρεσις.   [2] βούλησις.

nature of friendship depends on the character of the disposition of the friends. To make a friend of a person means that one regards him as an (apparent) good. The good man, when he makes a friend of another good man, has as his apparent good that which is really good for him: for a man who is good absolutely, when he becomes a friend to another good man, becomes a good relatively to him; *whereas an imperfect man is only good to his friend as means to what the other thinks good, and may not be good for him really. In the friendship of the good, then, the apparent good of each friend = what is really good for them = what is naturally good = the good man: only in the case of a person who possesses a determinate disposition can this equation be true. We see again, therefore, that a disposition is implied by friendship (and this consideration really serves to show the intimacy of the connection between friendship and virtue, inasmuch as the disposition which guarantees the truth of the equation is virtue—and the formation of a disposition of friendship depends, as we have seen, on the truth of the equation).*

Each friend, then, in the perfect friendship, possesses the 'friendly disposition' with reference to the other: each of them, then, fulfils the activities which proceed from this disposition. Not only does each *as we have seen* love that which is really good for him, but, *as the reciprocity of friendship implies*, he returns as much good to his friend, *both voluntarily*, in the good which he wishes him, and *involuntarily*, in the pleasure *which his society gives*. For the saying 'Friendship is equality' is most truly applied to the friendship of the good.

VI

We spoke before of the occurrence of friendship between persons who did not indulge in friendly intercourse: and we can now see how this can be. Among the sour-tempered, and those of an elderly habit of mind, friendship is found less often, and at a lower degree, precisely because, and in exact proportion as, they are worse-tempered—*i.e. less inclined to avoid giving pain to others*—and take less pleasure in social intercourse.[1] For an easy temper—*the desire to avoid giving pain*—and the active pleasure taken in social intercourse seem (*as we saw*) to be the marks most characteristic of friends. *Now we know that the activities which proceed from a disposition are precisely the same as those which go to form the disposition:* it follows that 'good temper and sociability' are the things which most tend to give rise to friendship, *for on them are based the activities of friendship. We know that the young live by the guidance of their emotions, seeking pleasure and shunning pain without reflection: and they do take pleasure in the company of others. The sour-tempered and elderly, on the other hand, do not.* This is why the young, *since they pursue the pleasure which other people can give,* form friendships—*or, more strictly, act as friends toward those who give them pleasure*—quickly, while the elderly, *who lack the incentive of pleasure and are prone to caution,* do not *form friendships quickly, but take a long time to form connections.* Men will not form friendships with persons

[1] αἱ ὁμιλίαι.

whose company gives them no pleasure, *because the
activity of friendship is based upon the pleasure taken in our
friends' company: and the elderly do not give one another any
pleasure.* (The same is true of those persons *of other ages*
who are sour-tempered.) *Men of this type may approve
of one another personally without deriving pleasure from one
another's society: and so they may form a disposition to wish each
other well, and render each other material services, without the
disposition to seek one another's company. Where they form
such a disposition,* we may say that they are 'well-disposed' to each other, inasmuch as they wish one another
well and rally to each other's assistance in case of need
—*two of the marks of friendship*—but they can hardly be
called 'friends', because their disposition, *though directed
towards each other personally and not incidentally, issues in
an activity which* lacks the daily intercourse and pleasure
in one another's company which, as we saw, are held
to be the greatest marks of friendship. *Their disposition
falls short of the disposition of friendship in precisely the same
respect as their liking for each other falls short of the liking
which true friends feel for each other.*

*Now that we know how men arrive at the perfect friendship,
we can see that* it is not possible to be friends, in the sense
implied by the perfect friendship, with many people:
it is the same with the perfect friendship as it is with
love:[1] one cannot be in love with many people at the
same time. Love seems to be an excess of emotion
(*whereas the emotion which gives rise to the perfect friendship
is not excessive, but of the right amount—one might say in*

[1] ἔρως.

illustration that the emotion of the elderly for one another is too small); and it is the nature of such excessive emotion that it be felt for one person, *which creates a presumption that one will be able to feel the emotion which gives rise to the perfect friendship for only a few people. This is true*—it is not easy for many persons to win very strong approbation from the same person (*and the affection of the perfect friendship is based upon very strong approbation*) at the same time: perhaps (*apart from this difficulty of man's inability to divide his attention*) we may also say that it is not easy for many people at the same time to be good, *as of course they must be to form the perfect friendship: for virtue is difficult. Further, the disposition of the perfect friendship takes a long time to form:* the friends must try each other by experience, and become thoroughly intimate with each other, *before they can know each other's character sufficiently well:* and it is very hard to see how one can live in such intimacy with many people.

This consideration affords us another difference between the perfect friendship and the other types: one can form 'friendships' for reasons of pleasure or profit with many people. The affection in such friendships is directed to the men only incidentally and not personally; so that for reasons of pleasure or profit many people[1] can win our approbation. In addition there are many people who can give us pleasure or profit: *the ability to do so does not depend upon a disposition of character to which only few can attain, as virtue does. Again,* the services of providing pleasure and utility do not take long (*whereas the intimacy required by*

[1] πολλοὺς Asp. Rr.

the perfect friendship does), *so that the grounds for these types of friendship can subsist between many people at the same time.*

This method of approach throws fresh light on the difference between the three types of friendship. We saw earlier that the type which is based upon pleasure bears a closer resemblance to the perfect friendship *than does the type which is based upon utility: and this is borne out by the fact that the type based on pleasure requires for its activity social intercourse—an activity far closer to that of the perfect friendship than the mere exchange of useful services which is the activity of the type based on utility. Further*, the resemblance *of the type based on pleasure to the perfect type* is at its highest when the two friends obtain the same things from each other: this they may do either by deriving pleasure from one another's character—*as two persons who are alike in respect of some good quality, such as two witty persons, may do*—or by taking pleasure in the same things. *In either case, the friends must come together to obtain their pleasure, and so give as much pleasure as they get: and their friendship is, as we have seen, more stable than that of persons who obtain different pleasures.* The friendships of the young, *which are usually based on pleasure of the latter type*, are a case in point. *In their delight in social intercourse with each other, such friends display an activity closely resembling that of the perfect friendship. People who pursue pleasure with such keenness are inclined to generosity towards the persons who give them the pleasure: for they do not weigh profit and loss in material things, but spend freely on their pleasures. So* in friendships of this nature, there is more liberality *between the friends than in the friendship that is based on utility:* the type that is based on utility is a thing for sordid souls, *who will not spend even on their friends unless they are sure of a profitable return. Even in the conferring of benefits, then, the friendship that is based on pleasure—and this is true, though to a lesser degree, of those who obtain different pleasures from the friendship—is closer to the activity of the perfect friendship than is the friendship that is based upon utility. We see its superiority* again *from the practice of* the supremely happy: *they* have no need of useful people, *and so do not form friendships for motives of utility,* but they do need pleasant people, *and so form friendships for motives of pleasure.* For they wish to live in companionship with someone, *as companionship is a natural need of human nature:* and they will put up with what is painful to them for a little while only—no one could put up with it continuously, not even with the Absolute Good, if it was painful to him. *Needing companionship, then, and being unable to live in companionship with the unpleasant,* the supremely happy therefore look out for friends who shall be pleasant. *So we see that the friendship which is based on pleasure does supply a need of human nature after a fashion, whereas that which is based on utility does not.* (Perhaps, *in order to obtain the highest blessings,* the supremely happy ought to look out for friends who are not only pleasant, but also good: if they could find friends who were good not only absolutely, but also relatively to them, they would have all the advantages *of pleasure and good* that friends should have. *But this last condition depends on their being good themselves: and that is another matter.*)

But though the perfect friendship does combine the ad-

vantages of the other two types with its own peculiar excellence, the other two types, depending as they do upon such different traits of character, are not often found in combination. This may be seen from the conduct of persons in positions of despotic rule (potentates), *who are free to choose whom they will. They* seem to have two distinct classes of friends: one set who are useful to them, and an entirely different set who are pleasant to them, the same persons being hardly ever in both sets. They do not, *when seeking friends for pleasure,* look for pleasant people who combine their pleasantness with virtue, *and so would be useful as well as pleasant:* nor do they, *when seeking friends for utility,* look for useful people whose utility is with a view to noble objects, *which are pleasant in themselves and would therefore ensure that the potentate obtained pleasure as well as profit from the friendship. On the contrary,* they seek on the one hand men who can satisfy their desire for pleasure by being e.g. witty, and on the other men who are clever at carrying out their instructions, *whether these are noble or not:* and these qualities are not often found in the same persons—*otherwise, the potentates would employ such persons. One might, perhaps, expect them to get out of their difficulty by making friends of good men:* as we have said before, the good man is both pleasant and useful. *We do not, however, find that they do so: and the reason lies in the good man's attitude to friendship.* A good man will not enter into friendship with a man in a position superior to his own, unless the superior in rank and power is also superior to him in merit.[1] *He knows*

---

[1] ἀρετή: 'virtue'.

that he cannot repay equal services to his superior in return for those which his superior confers on him, and that equality must be maintained in friendship. If, therefore, the superior in rank is not also superior to him in merit, the good man cannot put himself on an equal footing by being exceeded *in merit* in the same proportion as he is exceeded *in power: such superiority in merit could evoke in the good man a proportionate degree of respect and affection, which is the only coin in which the greater services could be repaid.* But potentates of this nature are not found every day: *so the good man, as he cannot of his own nature give respect and affection to anything other than merit, usually avoids them.*

But we are anticipating.—The friendships we have been discussing have been friendships of equality: *that is to say, we have assumed in our discussion of them that the friends in any given case are on the same footing.* The friends get the same things—*good, pleasure, or utility*—from each other, and wish the same things to each other: or else they effect a simple exchange of material assistance for pleasure: *virtue, of course, cannot be 'exchanged simply' for either profit or pleasure. We have assumed, in fact, that both friends are equally good, or else equally pleasant or useful to each other.*

(We have pointed out that the other types are less truly friendships *in their own nature*, and less permanent, than the perfect friendship. The difference of opinion as to whether they are friendships or not is due to their resemblance to and their difference from the same thing. In view of their resemblance to the perfect friendship they are held to be friendships, one possessing the element of pleasure, the other that of utility, both of which elements the perfect friendship also possesses: while in virtue of the fact that the perfect friendship is proof against calumny, and is permanent *of its own nature,* whereas they change quickly *whether there is outside interference or not,* and also have many other points of difference (*which we have seen*) from the perfect friendship—their difference from the perfect friendship gives rise to the view that they are not friendships at all. *Our own position, however, is perfectly clear: and we can henceforward ignore these questions.*)

VII

We can, however, make a further division of friendship, from another point of view: beside the 'friendships of equality' which we have been discussing, there is another class of friendship, *in which the two friends are not on the same footing, but* where one friend is superior *to the other (friendships of superiority). Clearly, it will make a great difference to friendship if one friend is superior to the other in goodness, pleasantness, or utility.* We may instance the relation in which a father stands to his son: *this is styled friendship, but the father is superior to the son, so that the friendship does not come under our previous discussion of friendship;* and in general, the relationship of an older to a younger man *is of this type, the relation father-son being a special instance of the superiority of an older to a younger man.* Similarly, there is the friendship of husband and wife: *here the husband is the ruling party;* in general, *then,* again, there is the relation of ruler to subject, *which will come under the head of 'friendships of superiority'.*

These 'friendships *of superiority*', however, *beside their obvious difference from the 'friendships of equality',* differ from each other as well, *according to the nature and the amount of the inequality between the friends (it may be, then, that we shall have to examine the separate instances of friendship of this type, in addition to laying down general rules).* The friendship of parents for their children is not the same as that of rulers for their subjects, *though actually parents do rule their children: only detailed examination of*

each of these friendships, then, will enable us to form con-
clusions concerning them. Further, there are even differences
within the individual friendships themselves: the friendship
of a father for his son is not the same as that of a son
for his father, nor is that of husband for wife the same
as that of wife for husband. *In these friendships, in fact,*
friendship is not an equally balanced and regularly reciprocal
relation. The reason is that *in these cases* the particular
excellence[1] of each party—the function, that is, *which*
each performs with regard to the other—is different: *this*
excellence is the reason or motive for the existence of the friend-
ship, and *therefore* the reason or motive of each party in
'loving' the other is different also. The affection *which*
each party inspires in the other is therefore different also:
and the friendship, *whether we consider it as a disposition*
formed in the one party for the other, or as a complex relation
existing between the two parties, is different likewise *in*
each case. It follows, then, that the friends do not obtain
the same things from each other, *as they do in the perfect*
friendship: nor, indeed, should they expect to obtain the
same things. *The duties which each owes to the other are*
determined by the relation in which each stands to the other: for
instance, when children render to their parents what
they ought to render to those who brought them into
the world, and parents render what they should to
their children, the friendship of such persons *has all that*
it should have, and will be abiding and excellent. *It*
would be manifestly absurd to expect either parents or children
to render the same things to each other, as we should expect

[1] ⟨ἡ⟩ ἀρετή Rs.

them to do if they were on an equal footing (ex hypothesi, in the case we gave, each is good): there are certain services which each ought to render to the other, but these are both different in kind and unequal in value. The element of equality which these friendships contain resides in the affection. Where one friend is superior to the other, the affection should in every case *be unequal* as well, *and should* be proportionate *to the relative merits of the parties.* That is to say, the one who is better, or more useful, or in any other way superior to the other, should be 'loved' more than he 'loves': *he should receive an amount of affection greater than that which he gives to the other in proportion to the extent of his superiority.* For when the affection is proportionate to the merit of the parties, then there is equality of a sort: and equality, as we have seen, is held to be characteristic of friendship.

The equality which obtains in this type of friendship, then, is an equality of ratios: and we saw previously, in our discussion of justice, that equality of ratios is the principle of justice; distributive justice[1] *in particular consisting in the appointment to each claimant of his dues in exact proportion to his merit.* But equality does not seem to hold the same place in acts of justice as it does in friendship. In acts of justice the *proportionate* equality which consists in the apportionment of claims according to merit is equality in the primary sense, while quantitative equality, *which consists in assigning to each claimant the same amount,* is equality only in a secondary sense. *That is to say, strict justice demands that two persons get their deserts, and is*

[1] τὸ διανεμητικὸν δίκαιον.

satisfied when they get their deserts, no matter how great the difference between them: only where they happen to be equal (or where, as in a democracy, they are treated as equals), is it just that they obtain the same things. In friendship, on the other hand, quantitative equality is the primary kind of equality, and proportion to merit is secondary. *That is to say, friendship is more perfect when the friends are equal, and obtain the same things (and the same quantity) from each other—in perfect friendship, in fact, the friends are completely equal. Where the friends are unequal, and the friendship is only proportional, the friendship is to that degree imperfect.* This is clear, if there is a great interval between the parties in goodness, badness, wealth, or any other respect. *Where the superiority of one party over the other is very great,* they are no longer friends—they do not, indeed, even expect to be friends: *for there can be proportionate equality, and therefore justice, between two persons, no matter how wide the interval between them, but friendship becomes impossible if the interval is too wide.* This is most clearly seen in the case of the gods: they surpass us most decisively in all good things, *and people obviously do not expect to enter into friendship with them, but offer them worship instead.* But it is also clear in the case of kings: with them, too, men who are much their inferiors in station do not expect to be friends. And no more do worthless persons expect to be friends with men of the greatest wisdom or merit.

These examples should make clear how far proportionate equality obtains in friendship. In such cases, it is impossible to give any accurate definition of the point up to which men are still friends, *and above which they cease to be friends. If, for instance, we take a pair of friends*, we may increase the gap between them by subtracting from one of the friends *so as to produce an ever-growing inequality between them*, yet the friendship still continues to exist: but when one of the pair has been removed to a great distance *from the other*, as God is *separated from us, we find that* the friendship exists no longer. *So we see that there is such a point, at which proportionate equality can no longer produce friendship: but mathematical accuracy cannot be expected in the study of human affairs, and this is one of the cases where our perception of individual cases has to be the sole method of determination.*

This, however, is the origin of the question, whether it is not after all untrue that friends wish each other the greatest of goods: does a man, for instance, wish his friends to become gods? *The argument is that* if they became gods, they would cease to be his friends, and therefore no longer be a good to him (for friends are goods): *so that to wish them to become gods is to wish to lose good oneself. Ex hypothesi, one cannot wish to lose good oneself; wish is directed toward what is good for oneself. The conclusion then is that one does not wish one's friends the greatest goods, but only such goods as are a means to our attainment of the greatest goods. This question, then, concerns the ultimate nature of the wish implied in friendship; does one, in making a friend of a good man, aim ultimately at securing good for oneself, or not? This cannot be answered here. We may say, however, in answer to the specific question raised—* assuming the correctness of the doctrine laid down, that a friend wishes good to his friend for the friend's sake—*that* such well-wishing is conditional upon the friend's remaining the person he is: his friend will wish him the greatest goods, but not such goods as will involve his ceasing to be a man—*he will wish him such goods as a man can enjoy.* And yet, perhaps, *there is something in the argument; and* he will not wish his friend all the greatest goods. It is for himself most of all that every man wishes what is good: *so that if there are any goods which, if he wishes his friend to have them, he must wish to lose himself, he will not wish them to his friend. But this question is too fundamental to be discussed here: and we must return to our 'friendships of superiority'.*

VIII

The majority of men, however, *in spite of the fact that quantitative equality is primary in friendship,* seem to wish to be loved rather than to love: and the reason for this is their love of honour.[1] Love of honour accounts for the fact that the majority of men like flattery: for the flatterer is a friend in an inferior position, or at least he pretends to be such, and *therefore* pretends to love more than he is loved—*which, as it is recognized that the inferior should love more than he is loved, gives his friend a comforting sense of his own superiority.* Being loved, *in fact,* seems to be nearly the same thing as being honoured: and most men, *as we saw,* aim at being honoured; *so that most men assume that being loved is the same thing as being honoured, and for that reason wish to be loved rather than to love.*

But being loved and being honoured are not quite the same thing. It appears that men do not seek after honour for its own sake, but incidentally: *their ultimate motive is something other than honour, and they seek honour because it happens to be a means to that thing.* For *instance,* most men like to be honoured by those in high positions: this is because of the hope *which honour from such a source inspires in them.* They think *when they meet with honour at the hands of the great that this means* that they will obtain from them whatever their particular need happens to be: they therefore enjoy the honour *in this case not for*

---

[1] φιλοτιμία.

its own sake, but as a token of benefits to come. *Another class of persons who pursue honour*, those who strive to obtain honour at the hands of good men and men of discernment (*men who know*), *do so because they* are trying to confirm their own good opinion of themselves: they therefore enjoy the honour they obtain, because they are enabled to believe that they are good by their confidence in the judgement of those who *by implication* say that they are. *These people also, then, seek to be honoured for the sake of something beyond the honour, and not for what it is in itself.*

It is this that constitutes the difference between being loved and being honoured. Men enjoy being loved for its own sake, *and not for any ulterior motive.* It would seem, then, that in this respect being loved is more valuable than being honoured: and, *inasmuch as being loved is an essential element in the complex of friendship*, we may conclude that friendship is worthy of choice for what it is in itself, *apart from any advantages which may be incidental to it.*

But *being loved, though it is an essential element in friendship, does not of itself constitute friendship: both parties must love, as well as be loved. In fact*, friendship seems to depend for its existence more on the loving than on the being loved: *for loving is an activity, whereas being loved is not, and loving therefore satisfies the needs of the human soul far more than being loved.*

The importance of loving in friendship may be seen from the pleasure which mothers take in loving their children. Some mothers give their children to other women to bring up, and know them for their own, and love them, but make no effort to secure a return of their affection from the children—this is in cases, of course, where they cannot *claim them for their own, and so* receive affection in addition to giving it. It seems to be sufficient for them to see their children well off; and they love their children even when the children do not know them, and therefore do not return to them any of the attentions and feelings due to a mother. *We cannot, of course, say that mother-love is the perfect friendship; their conduct in such cases seems in fact to be due to a natural instinct, not to a reasoned valuation of their children's merits. But the parental relation certainly comes under the head of friendship: and therefore the existence of the natural instinct in mothers to love their children, regardless of whether they are loved by them or not, is evidence that active loving, expressing a natural need, is the more important element in friendship.*

We may say, then,[1] that friendship consists more in the loving than in the being loved. In addition, *we see that* men praise those who show outstanding love for their friends: *and praise is awarded to those who exhibit a virtue, and may therefore be taken as indicating the presence of a virtue in the person praised.* Active loving therefore seems to be the virtue of friends: *that is to say, it is the rightness of his loving which distinguishes a good friend from a bad one.* Therefore where two friends love each other as each deserves to be loved, *the most essential psychological element in the friendship is satisfied, and* they are *therefore* attached to each other by a tie which is

_____
[1] δή. This appears to be an inference, not a fresh point.

lasting, and their friendship is lasting. *We saw previously on general grounds that the perfect friendship is lasting: and we can see now that the reason for this is that it
satisfies to the full the natural instinct to love what is good.*

So *in the friendships of superiority which we were discussing, we can see that* it is *by loving each other in accordance
with the merits of each* that unequal persons can render
their friendship most nearly akin to the perfect friendship. For they are equalized *when the superior loves the
inferior less, and the inferior loves the superior more, in proportion to the difference between them: and the force of the
equality lies in the love which each gives, far more than that
which he receives.*

*Equality is an old idea in friendship: and in fact, as the
old proverb has it,* 'equality and likeness are friendship';
*and we may now see how much truth there is in the contention
(cited in our review of previous opinions on friendship) that
friendship consists in likeness.* This is most true of those
who are alike in respect of virtue. For they are stable
in their essential natures; *and therefore, their acts and
their inclinations being consistently of the same type,* they are
also stable in relation to each other. They neither require base services nor render them, *so that neither has
any reason to alter the regard which he feels for the other:* on
the contrary, they may even be said to restrain one
another *from base actions, and so to maintain one another
in the stable path of virtue:* for it is characteristic of the
good that they neither err themselves nor permit their
friends to err.

The base, on the other hand, *though they are alike in*

the fact that they are base, have no stability in friendship: for they do not remain even like themselves for long, *much less like each other.* They do become friends, but only for a short time, as each rejoices in the other's badness. *For while every man takes pleasure in acts of the same kind as his own, badness involves interests and pleasures of such varying kinds that two such persons cannot coincide in pleasing each other for long.*

There is more permanence in the friendship of those whose motive is utility or pleasure: it lasts as long as they provide each other with profit or pleasure. *Persons who are alike in pursuing profit or pleasure of a normal kind are usually consistent ('like themselves') in doing so: and the interest or pleasure of two such persons may therefore coincide for a considerable time.*

We also cited, in our review of previous opinions on friendship, the view opposed to that which we have just discussed, namely that friendship is a union of opposites. In human friendship, it is the friendship whose motive is utility which seems most easily capable of arising between opposites: the friendship of a poor for a wealthy man, or of an ignorant for a learned man, may serve as examples. *Where men are possessed of opposed qualities such as these, they may join in friendship for the sake of utility:* for a man aims at securing the particular thing which he happens to lack, *so joins in friendship with the man who possesses it,* and gives *him* something else in exchange.

Under this head, *however, if we wished to be pedantic,* we might force the friendship of the lover and the beloved, or of the beautiful and the ugly—*examples which, as we saw earlier in the case of the former pair, come from the friendship whose motive is pleasure, but where the parties obtain different pleasures and might, therefore, be represented as being in some sense opposites. If we apply the principle of proportionate exchange established in the previous chapter,* we can see how it is that lovers sometimes appear ridiculous, when they claim to be loved as much as they love. *When the beloved can obtain from them as much as they obtain from the beloved—i.e.* when they are equally lovable with the beloved—perhaps their claim is justified, *for otherwise the friendship will be unbalanced:* but when (*as not infrequently happens*) they have no such support for their claim, it is absurd.

This principle that opposites desire their opposites, (and also the principle that like seeks like,) has been erected into a principle of universal operation. Perhaps, however, it is not even true that opposite desires its opposite for what is in itself, but that it desires it incidentally, desire being of the mean state *to which it can attain by union with the opposite.* For it is the mean state which *in every case* is good, *and therefore desirable absolutely:* for example, it is not the good of the dry that it become wet, but that it should arrive at the mean state, *and it desires the wet because by union with the wet it can arrive at the mean state between wet and dry;* and the same may be said of *the desire of* the hot *for the cold,* and of the other natural opposites. But we had better leave these enquiries: they do not belong to our subject, *which is the study of human conduct, but* to *physics.*

IX

At the very beginning *of our discussion of friendship*, we asserted its connection with justice: *and this connection is a fact, for* it seems that friendship is indeed concerned with the same sphere of actions, and exists between the same persons, as justice. For in every community[1]— *between every set of persons who are united by a common objective or a common interest*—there is *commonly* held to be some form of justice—*some specific conduct that is just, in that the members have the right to expect such conduct of each other;* and *it seems that there is* friendship also: at any rate, men address their fellow-sailors and fellow-soldiers as friends, and likewise those who are associated with them in the other forms of community. *Popular opinion and popular practice, then, seem to show that friendship and justice are both found between any and every set of persons who are united in a community.*

Moreover friendship exists between the members of a community to exactly the same extent as they are associated in the community: *there is some evidence for this in the fact that* justice also exists to exactly the same degree—*i.e. the object and the closeness of the community between any set of persons determines the extent and the nature of the rules which govern their conduct toward each other, and we may therefore conclude that it will determine the closeness of the bond of friendship which exists between them.* The proverb which says 'the property of friends is common'

[1] κοινωνία: 'association', 'partnership'.

is right: for friendship can only exist between those who are in a community *of some sort—i.e. between those who have something in common.*

Now brothers and comrades, *between whom there is clearly a very strong bond of friendship,* have everything in common. In the other communities, on the other hand, the amount which the members have in common is in each case determined *by the type and purpose of the community in question, and differs accordingly*—they may have more or less in common: and in fact, the *tie of* friendship as well is *stronger or weaker in the various communities, and is therefore* more or less worthy of the name of friendship. *Facts, then, seem to show that the holding of common interests and friendship go hand in hand.*

But it is not only the tie of friendship which differs as between the members of the various communities: the conduct which is prescribed as just differs also. It is not the same, for instance, between parents and children as it is between brothers, nor is it the same between comrades as it is between fellow-citizens; and the same is true of the other friendships (*for as community implies friendship, we may describe the bond between these persons by either name indifferently*). *In each case there is certain conduct which is prescribed as just.* It follows that the type of conduct which is accounted unjust in each friendship is different also: and *it is an observed fact that* unjust conduct is accounted the more unjust, the closer the tie of friendship which binds the parties together. It is a more terrible thing, for instance, to defraud a comrade of money than it is to defraud a fellow-citizen; *while justice forbids us to defraud a fellow-citizen, it is the strength of the positive tie of friendship between comrades that renders such conduct between them correspondingly more terrible.* It is a more terrible thing, also, to refuse aid to a brother, than to refuse it to a stranger: and a more terrible thing to strike one's father than to strike anyone else at all. It is the nature of justice that the obligation to perform such actions as are just increases in strength exactly as the friendship between the parties is stronger: and our original contention, that friendship and justice exist between the same persons, and are of equal extension in the field of action, was therefore strictly accurate.

This being so, we can see that friendship must play some part in the mutual relations of citizens. All other communities may be compared to parts of an organic whole—the political community (*the community of the city*). *To take an instance,* men travel together (*and therefore form a community*) on condition that they reap some particular advantage—to procure, *it may be,* some one of the necessities of life: and advantage is commonly held to be the motive which originally prompted, and continues to maintain, the union of men in the political community. The lawgivers show this, when they make such laws as will conduce to the advantage of the city, and when they say that the code of conduct which they prescribe as just is just precisely because it is to the common advantage. *As the common advantage of the citizens, then, includes the particular advantage of the members of the separate communities, so the community of the city in-*

cludes the other communities as an organic whole includes its parts. Now the other communities aim at advantage piecemeal: fellow-sailors, for instance, aim at the particular advantage to be gained by their voyage—money-making or the like—and fellow-soldiers aim at the particular advantage to be gained from the war in which they are engaged, whether their object be to gain money, to defeat the enemy, or to capture a city; while fellow-tribesmen and fellow-demesmen, similarly, aim at the particular advantage to be gained *by local government.* All these communities seem *on the face of it* to be subordinate to the political community: *they aim each at the individual and momentary advantage that is set before them, whereas* the political community aims not at the advantage of the moment, but at the advantage which covers the whole *extent and* period of a man's life.

Some[1] of the individual communities, however, seem to be formed for *nothing more than* the pleasure of their members, *and might therefore seem to be exceptions to this rule:* we may instance religious guilds[2] and social clubs.[3] These have as their object the performance of sacrifices, and companionship, the members holding sacrifices and gatherings for that purpose, whereby they give due honours to the gods, and provide relaxation, combined with pleasure, for themselves. *The honouring of the gods is clearly of advantage to the state; and relaxation is a means to the more competent performance of man's more serious*

---

[1] Bywater, in *J. of Phil.* xvii, p. 69; J. Cook Wilson, in *C.R.* xvi, 1902, p. 28.
[2] θιασῶται.   [3] ἐρανισταί.

occupations, so that these communities contribute to the aim of the political community. That the ultimate aim of such gatherings is relaxation, is shown by the fact that the sacrifices and gatherings which have come down to us from ancient times seem to be held after the harvesting of the crops, and are of the nature of offerings of first-fruits: the reason being that in the old days men had most leisure at those times.

Those communities which seem to have pleasure in view are therefore seen to serve the end of the political community. All the different communities therefore seem to be parts of the political community, *so that they should all subserve the greater end to which they contribute.* And, *as community implies friendship, we may say as a general rule that* the type and strength of the friendship between members of any given community will correspond to the character of the community.

X

It follows that there will be friendship between the members of any state, and that the friendship will differ in strength and in type according to the constitution of the state. We shall do well, then, to call to mind the characteristics of the various types of constitution.

There are three types of constitution *which may be taken as normal,* and three *which we may call* 'deflections' *from the normal,* being as it were perversions of the three normal constitutions. The *normal* constitutions are first kingship, second aristocracy (*we may class these two together because in both the rule is in the hands of the best persons—of one man in kingship, of several in aristocracy*); the third is that which is based upon a property classification, which it seems appropriate to call 'timocratic' (*deriving the sense from assessment,*[1] *in spite of the use of the term by other persons (e.g. Plato) in a sense derived from honour*[2]); though the majority of people are in the habit of calling it 'constitutional government' simply. Of these three constitutions kingship is the best, and 'timocracy' the worst.

The 'deflection' from kingship is tyranny. Both kingship and tyranny consist in the rule of one man, but there is a very wide difference between them, in that the tyrant looks to his own advantage, *and not to that of his subjects,* while the king looks to the advantage of his subjects. *We do not mean that the king is merely dis-*

---

[1] τίμημα.　　　　　　　[2] τιμή.

interested: a monarch is not a king if he is not self-sufficient, and superior to his subjects in all good things. A man in such a position and of such a character cannot stand in need of anything to complete his well-being: and therefore he will not look to his own advantage, *for material gain means nothing to him,* but he will look to the advantage of his subjects *in order to give expression to his virtues.* A man who *holds the sole sovereignty, if he* is *disinterested but* lacking in the pre-eminent qualities of the king as we have described him, *can neither discern nor obtain the advantage of his subjects, and* is *therefore* a king only in name, like the 'kings' who are elected by lot, *and do not perform the functions of kings.*

Tyranny is the exact opposite of this: *for whereas the king looks to what is good absolutely, and thereby secures what is good for his subjects,* the tyrant looks to what is good for himself, *which is not good absolutely and can only be attained at the expense of others—his subjects.* It is more obvious that tyranny is the worst of constitutions *than it is that kingship is the best. The badness of tyranny is attested by all: and we may add to our bare statement of the pre-eminence of kingship a logical proof:—*The worst is that which is opposite to the best, *and conversely, the best is that which is opposite to the worst: kingship is opposite to tyranny, the worst constitution, therefore kingship is the best constitution. No one, of course, would choose to be ruled by a tyrant: but we called the perverted forms of constitution by the musical term 'deflections' because they represent a form which can be reached by a change in the arrangement of a normal form. In spite of tyranny being its opposite,* a state can arrive at tyranny from kingship: tyranny is a base form of the rule of one man, and a king who is wicked *therefore* turns to a tyrant.

The 'deflection' from aristocracy is oligarchy: and the change from aristocracy to oligarchy comes about through the badness of the rulers. It happens when they apportion the good things of the state (*the rewards and privileges*) contrary to the merit of the citizens: they allot all or most of the good things to themselves, and *therefore* give the offices always to the same persons, accounting wealth, *not merit*, the highest qualification *for office, as well as the object of holding office*. It follows that the government, instead of being in the hands of the best people (*in an aristocracy, they may be many or few, but obtain office solely by their merits*), is in the hands of a few men of base character: *and this constitutes oligarchy*.

The 'deflection' from timocracy is democracy: so the natural change from timocracy is to democracy. *The change is simple, because* these two constitutions are co-terminous: *that is to say*, timocracy as well as democracy has the ideal of the rule of the majority, and, *whereas in democracy all men have equal privileges, provided only that they are free*, *in timocracy* all those who are within the required assessment have equal rights. Democracy, *though it is a perversion*, is the least bad *of the three 'deflections'*, inasmuch as the deflection from the *normal form of* constitution, *timocracy*, is only small.

These, then, are the constitutions of states; and these are the ways in which changes most tend to take place in the constitutions. The changes we have described are the smallest which can occur, and *therefore* come about most easily. *And we can gain further knowledge of them from the consideration of social phenomena.* We can find likenesses—as it were, patterns—of the constitutions existing in the individual households.

The community[1] of a father with his sons bears the form of kingship: for the father cares for the welfare of his sons, *as the king cares for the welfare of his subjects.* And this is why Homer calls Zeus, *the king of the universe,* 'father Zeus': the ideal of kingship, *in which one who is wiser and better than his subjects cares for their welfare,* being paternal rule.

The 'deflection', tyranny, also occurs in the households. Among the Persians, the community of the father *with his sons* is tyrannical: they treat their sons as slaves. The community of a master with his slaves *in a normal household* may also be taken as an example of tyrannical rule: it is the advantage of the master, *not of the slaves,* that is secured in it, *just as it is the advantage of the tyrant, not his subjects, that is secured in a city. A slave is a living tool, and exists for the sake of his master's advantage alone, so that* in the case of the master and slaves the tyrannical community seems to be the proper form: in the case of the Persian father and his sons, it seems wrong, *as the son has the right to expect care from his father.* Different things—*as sons and slaves*—should be ruled differently.

---

[1] The translation 'association' seems to be nearer to the sense: but I preferred to use 'community', since Aristotle is obviously conscious throughout of the derivation of κοινωνία from κοινόν, and it seemed preferable to use the English 'community' and so keep connection with 'common'.

Aristocracy also may be seen in the households: the community of man and wife seems to bear the character of an aristocracy. It is according to merit—*as in an aristocracy*—that the man is the ruling party: that is to say, he rules in those matters which it befits the man to order, and gives to his wife *the rule in* those matters which are fitting for a woman.

The 'deflection' of aristocracy, oligarchy, may be seen in the community of man and wife as well: when the husband controls everything, he changes the community from aristocracy to oligarchy. It is contrary to merit that he controls everything; that is to say, that such control is not based on his superiority, *as there are things in which he is not superior to his wife.* Sometimes, again, the wife rules everything—as happens when she is an heiress: *and she, too, is ruling then in matters wherein she is inferior to her partner.* In these cases, then, the rule does not go by excellence, *as in aristocracy*, but by wealth and power, as happens in oligarchies.

We can also find timocracy in the households: the community of brothers *in the management of one household* resembles that of timocracy: the brothers are equal, *and in virtue of their common birth have privileges superior to those of the other members—the slaves, for instance.* The difference in age between the brothers does indeed produce a corresponding inequality in authority between them: *and thus far there is a difference between the community of brothers and timocracy. But generally speaking, brothers have equal authority within the household:* and that is why, if the difference in age between them is very great, the friendship between them, *which of course corresponds in character to the community,* is no longer fraternal, *since the difference in age precludes the equality which should be characteristic of the friendship of brothers.*

We can find the closest parallel to *the deflection from timocracy,* democracy, in those habitations (*one can hardly call them households*) where there is no master: there all the members are on equal terms, *and there is therefore a parallel to democracy, where all free men are equal.* We may also find democracy (*though the parallel is less exact*) in those households where the ruler is weak, and every member can *therefore* do as he likes.

XI

Each of these constitutions may be seen to involve friendship to exactly the same extent as it involves justice: *as each constitution involves a different type of conduct which is accounted just, so it will involve a different type of friendship. This will become clear if we examine our instances.*

The friendship which exists between a king and his subjects is determined by the benefits which he confers upon them, which far exceed those which they confer upon him: *so that the friendship is one of superiority, in the sense previously defined.* The king does confer benefits on his subjects, *while himself receiving very little,* since he is good—*and can therefore discern what is good for them*—and tends them simply with a view to their welfare, just as a shepherd tends his sheep. (This parallel explains why Homer spoke of Agamemnon as 'shepherd of the people'.)

The friendship between a father and his sons is of the same type, *being determined by the benefits conferred by the father on the sons: but it is not exactly the same as that between a king and his subjects.* The father confers greater benefits on his sons than the king on his subjects; *and this, of course, makes a difference to the friendship.* The father is the author of his sons' existence, which is held to be the greatest of boons, and of their nurture and education. *His position is similar to that of the ancestors of the family; and the reverence in which ancestors are held shows the relation of superiority in which they stand to their descendants. The reason for the reverence is that* these same benefits[1]— *existence, nurture, and education*—are attributed to the ancestors, as well *as to the father.*

A further reason for the character of the friendship in these three cases is that it is natural for it to be of this type. It is natural for a father to rule his sons, for ancestors to rule their descendents, and for a king to rule his subjects: *and the ruler is of course in a position of superiority to the ruled.*

These three friendships, then, are 'friendships of superiority'. And this is the reason why parents receive honour *as well as service from their children: honour being the only thing with which the children can, in accordance with the principles established in our discussion of 'friendships of superiority', requite the superior benefits which their parents have bestowed on them. Further, as the type of conduct which can be claimed as just varies with the type of friendship in every community,* it follows that in these communities the claims of justice are not the same for ruler and ruled, but are proportionate to merit—*the ruler can claim more from the ruled than vice versa*—this being the principle which is operative also in the friendship between these persons.

The friendship of man and wife is the same as that which exists in an aristocracy. *As each party rules in turn according to their merit, so likewise* the friendship is determined by their goodness, the better party receiving more *affection*[2] *than the worse,* and each being awarded what is befitting *to his or her peculiar excellence.*

---

[1] ταὐτὰ Rs. προσνέμεται.   [2] [ἀγαθόν] secl. Rm.

The claims of justice are regulated by the same principle—*which confirms our remarks concerning the friendship.*

The friendship between brothers is like that between comrades, *whose character is already known to us.* Brothers are on an equal footing with one another, and are much of an age; and those who are in this position are generally speaking alike in their feelings and character. The friendship which is found in timocracy—*the constitution which we saw had its parallel in the relations of brothers—naturally* also resembles that of comrades. The ideal of timocracy is that the citizens be equal, all being good men (*not, of course, men of supreme excellence, but of a reasonable degree of goodness*); and for this reason, *assuming that all the citizens are alike in their merits,* they take it in turn to rule, and are all on an equal footing. *The friendship here, then, is not between rulers and ruled, but between the whole body of the citizen populace: and* therefore, *since all are on an equal footing,* the friendship likewise is of the type obtaining between equals.

In the 'deflections', however, just as justice exists only to a small extent—*as these constitutions represent a violation by the rulers of the natural forms of human unions, there is hardly any conduct which the rulers have the right to expect from the ruled*—so too there is friendship *between rulers and ruled* only to a small extent. This is most true of the worst of the deflections: in tyranny there is little or no friendship *between ruler and ruled.*

The reason for this lies in the principle previously established, that friendship and justice can only exist between persons who have something in common: where there is nothing in common between ruler and ruled, there is no friendship either—nor, in fact, is there any justice. We may instance the relation in which a craftsman stands to his tool, the soul to the body, or a master to his slave. In all these cases, the inferior party derives benefit from the care bestowed upon it by its user. But *it is obvious that,* in the case of the inanimate objects *at least,* there is no friendship between them and their users, nor is there any justice—*they obviously have no right to expect any treatment other than that which conduces to the user's profit. It is impossible to speak of the existence of a common interest, where the one party exists simply to subserve the interest of the other, and is simply a means to the attainment of that interest. We may extend this from inanimate tools to animate ones;* there is no more friendship between its owner and a horse or an ox, *than if it were an inanimate tool;* or even between master and slave, qua slave. *The reason is the same:* they have nothing in common. A slave is a living tool, and a tool is an inanimate slave, *and in this capacity they stand in precisely the same relation to their employer.*

We may, however, make a reservation in the case of the slave: qua slave, there can be no friendship between him and his master (*or, of course, any other free man*), but qua man, there may be. It is an accepted opinion that there is justice of some sort (*some sort of conduct which is just in the sense that it can be claimed as a right*) in every case between a man and any being who can share in a system of law or be a party to an agreement—*and a slave, being a man, must come under this head:* and it follows *from the principle of the equal extension of friendship and justice,* that one can have friendship for a slave, in so far as he is a man.

It follows, then, *from the principle that friendship and justice can only exist between persons who have something in common,* that in political tyrannies, as well *as the domestic tyrannies analysed above,* there is friendship and justice *between ruler and ruled* only to a small extent: whereas in democracy they exist to a larger extent *than in the other deflections.* Where men are equal, *as they are in a democracy,* they have many things in common: *so that in a democracy, there is a corresponding degree of friendship— not between rulers and ruled merely, but between all the citizens.*

XII

All friendship, then, involves *some sort of* community *between the parties*—as has previously been said: *and we might therefore represent the different types of friendship as so many different species, corresponding to the different species of community.* One might, however, make the friendship of kinsmen and of comrades into separate species *from 'communal friendship'*[1] *in the strict sense.* The friendships that exist between fellow-citizens, fellow-tribesmen, and fellow-sailors, and members of similar communities, *are defined in their character in each case by the purpose of the particular community, which is a clearly stated object whose nature dictates the conduct of the members toward one another; and therefore these friendships* are more like communal friendships *in the strict sense than the friendships of kinsmen and of comrades.* They seem to rest upon a sort of *external* contract, *whereas the friendship of kinsmen and of comrades does not: so the distinction is a proper one for the purpose of our discussion.*

Since this is the character of communal friendship proper, one might class among the communal friendships the friendship of host and guest,[2] *which is manifestly determined by an overt contract. There are, then, as many species of communal friendship proper as there are communities determined by such a contract for a definite purpose.*

The friendship of kinsmen, too, seems to admit of division into several species, *inasmuch as there are many*

---

[1] ἡ κοινωνικὴ φιλία.　　　　[2] ἡ ξενικὴ φιλία.

different grades of kinship. All these different species depend on the friendship between parent and child, *from which they are in fact derived. The fact that the child is derived from the parent is the source to which all the varieties of kinship may be traced.* Parents love their children as being some part of themselves, while children love their parents as themselves being something derived from their parents. *The fact that the child is derived from the parent is the basis of their friendship; but as it affects them differently, so the friendship which each has for the other is different also. The friendship of parents for their children is far greater than the friendship which their children have for them: and for this three reasons may be given.*

First, parents know the children that are sprung from them for their own far better than their offspring know that they are sprung from their parents.

Second, the party which is the origin of the other feels its identity with its offspring far more deeply than the product feels its identity with its producer. The producer, or source, feels that the product belongs to it—e.g. the man to whom a tooth, or a hair, or anything else *of the kind* belongs, feels that it is his—whereas the product has no such feeling for the producer, or has it in a less degree.

Third, the duration of the friendship is greater *on the side of the parents than on the side of the children.* The parents love the children as soon as they come into being, but a certain time must elapse before the children attain the power of understanding, or *at least* of discrimination by the senses, and *so are able to* love their parents.

We may note in passing that these considerations, in addition *to showing why parents love their children more than their children love them,* make clear the reasons why mothers love their children more *than fathers do.*

The fact that the child comes from the parent as its source, then, is fundamental in the friendship of parent and child: and from this friendship the other friendships of kinship are derived. Parents love their children as themselves (their issue being, as it were, their 'other selves'—'other' in virtue of their separate existence, '*selves*', *as explained above, in virtue of their origin*): and children love their parents as the source from which they have grown.

Brothers *derive their friendship from this same fact: they* love one another in virtue of their common origin in the same source. *That is to say,* their identity with their source makes them feel their identity with one another. (This is the origin of the phrases 'the same blood', 'the same root', and the like, *which are used of brothers and kinsmen generally.*)

They are, then, in a sense the same thing, though in different individuals. *But there are, of course, other reasons for the closeness of their friendship as well: as we have seen,* it makes very strongly for friendship that they are brought up together and are of an age: *as the proverbs have it,* 'two of an age agree', and 'familiarity makes comrades'. This *similarity of tastes and character between brothers* is the reason why the friendship of brothers is held to resemble that of comrades.

The feeling of cousins and kinsmen of the other degrees that they belong to one another is derived from *the friendship of* brothers: it arises from the fact that they come from the same source. And kinsmen feel that this tie is closer or looser in proportion as they are more or less near to the original ancestor.

This, then, is the ultimate origin of the various friendships of kinship: and we may now make a few remarks concerning their general characteristics. The friendship which children have for their parents—and likewise that which men have for gods—is directed toward its object because that object is good, and *in fact* exceeds them in goodness. *As we have seen,* their parents have conferred on them the greatest of goods, in being responsible for their existence and nurture, and after their birth for their education. *They therefore attribute superior goodness to their parents: and so far, goodness is the motive of the friendship, which will also exhibit the characteristics of 'friendships of superiority'.* The friendship of parent and child further contains both pleasure and utility, and contains both of these things to a greater extent than the friendship between persons who are unrelated—greater to the same degree as parent and child live their life more in common, *and therefore share their pleasures and their profits more, than strangers do.*

The friendship of brothers, too, has the same characteristics as are found in the friendship of comrades. (*We may take comrades as the type par excellence of persons who enter into friendship for no other reason than personal choice, and are otherwise unrelated: and we saw in our preliminary analysis of friendship that where two such persons are good, their friendship contains good, pleasure and utility.*

We have also seen the part played in such friendships by likeness of tastes and character.) It has them to a greater degree (*than the friendship of comrades*) when the brothers are good: *for goodness, as we have seen, heightens the other characteristics of all friendship.* Generally speaking, indeed, it has them to a greater degree when the brothers are alike *in other respects than goodness*—greater inasmuch as brothers feel more deeply that they belong to one another, having started with a love for one another from their birth, and as those who (*like brothers*) are born of the same parents, and are brought up together in the same house, and are educated alike, are more alike in their character *than other people. A further point of superiority in the friendship of brothers lies in the fact that as they have lived all their lives together*, the 'test of time', *of which we spoke in an earlier chapter*, is most complete in their case, and *so* produces the strongest possible conviction.

In the kinsmen of the other grades, *as their friendship is derived from the friendship of brothers*, *so* the characteristics of their friendship are in each case proportionate *to the closeness of the blood-relationship.*

The friendship of man and wife, *which of course belongs in a sense to the friendship of kinship*, *seems also to fall outside the definition of communal friendship: it* seems to be due to a natural instinct. For *while the city is the end of the human community*, man is by nature a pairing animal rather than a political animal, inasmuch as the household—*the result of his pairing*—is prior in time to the city, and must in fact exist in order that the city may exist (*while the converse is not true*), and inasmuch as the begetting of children—*the motive of his pairing*—is shared with the other animals to a greater extent *than are the actions which form the end of the community of the city. The friendship of man and wife, then, may be said to be due primarily to a natural instinct, and not to an overt contract made for a clearly defined end: and yet the results of this friendship are not confined to the fulfilling of the merely animal instincts.* The other animals enter into community only so far as is necessary for reproduction, whereas man and woman do not live together only for the sake of reproduction, but also for the fulfilment of the other purposes of life. This may be seen from the fact that their natural functions are different from the start, those of man being different from those of woman: *and* therefore *they can better attain the larger ends of common life by union in the household.* Each contributes to the other's welfare, contributing his or her individual gifts to the common store. And the varied nature of their contributions is the reason why their friendship is held to involve both utility and pleasure. *These need not, however, be the only motive for the friendship (to work again for a moment in the categories of our original analysis of friendship).* If both man and wife are good, the motive of the friendship may be virtue as well: for there is a virtue that is peculiar to each of them, so that each may delight in the other's virtue. (*We may note that they will not be alike in virtue, though their friendship is based on virtue.*)

The bond between man and wife, *which holds them*

in a lasting friendship even though they are dissimilar, seems to consist in their children. This is why, where they have no children, they tend to part more easily. Their children are a good which is common to both of them: and the possession of something in common, *as we have seen,* forms a bond between people.

Now the conduct which is appropriate between the members of these various friendships will of course be different: and, in view of our recent discussion of the inter-relation of friendship and justice, we may now sum up the matter by saying that the question 'How should a man live in relation to his wife?'—the general question, in fact, 'How should a friend live in relation to his friend?' seems to mean just this—'What specific conduct is just between the parties in question?' The claims of justice do not seem to be the same between a man and his friend as they are between the same man and a stranger, nor are they the same between *friends of different degrees, such as* comrades and schoolfellows: *the nature of the friendship in every case determines certain conduct between the parties, and that conduct is just.*

XIII

Having established this conclusion, we may now examine some concrete examples of conduct between friends, and see whether we can obtain any guidance for our conduct in such cases. So far, our discussion has been mainly theoretical, but we must not forget that our aims are practical. It will be more convenient for our discussion if we call to mind briefly the results of our earlier discussion.

There are, as has been stated at the commencement of our discussion, three friendships, *or species of friendship, the basis of these being good, pleasure and utility respectively:* and in each of these the friends may either be on equal terms, or one may be superior to the other. *There are, then, six possible types of friendship: in the friendship that is based on virtue,* the friends may be equally good, or a better man may be the friend of a worse; and likewise, in the friendship that is based on pleasure *the friends may be equally pleasant or one may be more pleasant than the other,* and in the friendship that is based on utility they may be equal or unequal in the benefits they confer. *We pass over for the moment the friendship produced by the exchange of profit for pleasure, though here too the parties may be on an equal or an unequal footing. Further, we have seen that friendship demands that equality be maintained between the parties: so that* those who are equal *in the quality which is the basis of the friendship* must preserve equality by rendering the affection and the other friendly offices to each other on the basis of strict equality; while those who are unequal must preserve it by rendering these things[1] in proportion to their respective superiority and inferiority.

The preservation of equality, then, should ensure that friendship will run smoothly: and we may draw some useful practical lessons from the examination of the cases in which it does not run smoothly. As in our previous discussion, we will take first the friendship of equals.

The complaints and reproaches *which we see between friends* occur in the friendship whose motive is utility— either in this alone or at all events to a greater extent than in any other type of friendship. This might be expected, *as an examination of the other two types will show—we will again postpone consideration of the 'mixed' type.*

Men who base their friendship on virtue are each eager to do good to the other: doing good to one's friends is *acknowledged to be* characteristic of virtue and friendship, *i.e. a good friend, as we saw, will do good to his friend for the friend's sake, not for his own.* As they compete with each other, then, in conferring, *not in obtaining,* benefits, there is no room for complaints or quarrelling between them. *They cannot come either from the donor or from the recipient. The recipient has no cause for complaint,* for no one objects to a man who regards him as a friend and shows his regard by doing good to him: on the contrary, if he is a man of good feeling he takes his revenge by doing good *to his benefactor, so that neither party can complain that he loses anything.* The one who out-

[1] τῷ τὸ Coraes.

does the other, again, obtains the object at which he aims *by his beneficence, namely the good of his friend,* and so will have no complaint against his friend. Every man aims at what is good: *and the good friend obtains what is good in doing good to his friend.* (*The psychological reason for this will be discussed later.*)

The friendship that is based upon virtue, then, does not admit of complaints or quarrelling: and they can hardly occur in the friendship that is based upon pleasure, either. Both parties at once obtain what they are aiming at *in their friendship, i.e. pleasure:* if they take a delight in spending their time together, *the fact of their doing so must provide them with the pleasure they seek.* And here again *the donor has no reason for complaint;* it would seem absurd for a man to complain that his friend gives him no pleasure, *while he does give his friend pleasure.* He is under no compulsion to spend his time in his friend's company, *so that if he does so and gets no return for the pleasure he gives, he has only himself to blame.*

The friendship that is based upon utility, however, does give rise to complaints: *and it is clear from the nature of the friendship that there is need for discrimination in the conduct which it entails.* The friends *do not* associate with each other *for each other's sakes, but* for profit, and therefore are always wanting to get more *than they give:* they are always thinking that they are getting less than their due, and *therefore* each reproaches his partner on the grounds that he does not get as much as he wants and deserves. *The recipient, in fact, is never satisfied that he has got enough: while the donor does not feel satisfied with his part.* Those who do good *to persons whose motive is profit* cannot supply as much as the recipients want, *and would have to be for ever giving, without getting the return which ex hypothesi they seek.*

This being the general character of those who engage in this type of friendship, it is natural that disputes should arise in it: a closer analysis of the friendship itself will throw further light upon how they arise, and upon the conduct which is appropriate to it. Now we know that there are two kinds of justice: *conduct may be just either because it conforms to certain rules which are* unwritten *but are nevertheless valid,* or *because it is* in conformity with *the prescriptions of written* law. It seems that we have here a parallel with the friendship that is based upon utility: there being likewise two types of this, one of which is 'moral'— *i.e. it depends for its fulfilment, not upon a written contract, but upon the character of the parties*—and the other legal— *i.e. it depends upon a written (or otherwise stated) contract between the parties. In the former of these, the return is made when and as the 'debtor' pleases: in the latter, it is stipulated.* Complaints therefore arise most of all when the parties do not dissolve their association according to the same type of friendship as that under which they entered it— *i.e. when a man who has laid another under a 'moral' obligation demands his return as though it were a 'legal' obligation.*

This is obviously to be avoided. But we may now examine separately the two types of this friendship, and see what conduct is appropriate in each.

The 'legal' type is the friendship that is on fixed terms; *and of this we may make two further subdivisions.* The

first is purely a matter of business, *in which the parties
effect a simple exchange of services* from hand to hand: *there
is no room here for disagreement as to the obligations of either
party.* The second is more liberal, in that the return is
not made *on the spot, but* after a certain interval (*which
need not, of course, be fixed*): but here *too* there is an agreement (*not necessarily a written agreement*) as to the quid
pro quo. Here, *too*, the debt between the two parties is
quite clear, and does not admit of dispute. *In fact, both
these types of association hardly merit the name of friendship,
if it is to be used in its proper sense:* the friendly element *in
the second type* consists in the postponement. *As we saw,
a true friend confers benefits upon his friend without asking for
any return at all: so that if one trusts a man to make a return
later, one is acting as a friend in not demanding payment on
the spot.* And this is why in some systems of society there
is no provision for legal enforcement of claims in these
cases: they think that those who have entered into
associations on the basis of credit should put up with
the results of their actions—*they have treated their partner
as a friend, and should not rely upon legal aid in dealing with
their friends.*

The 'moral' type is not on fixed terms: *there is no
definite agreement as to the return to be made.* One party
makes a gift, or does whatever other service it may be,
to the other as to a friend: *when the gift is made, in fact,
he adopts the attitude of the true friend, who as we saw performs his services solely in order to benefit his friend.* But
*this is not his true motive, which is to gain profit for himself:
and therefore* he expects to receive in return as much as

he gave, or more, on the grounds that it was not a gift but a loan. If *his friend understands this, all will be well: but if his friend does not, and* he comes out of the association worse off than when he entered into it, he will complain *that he has been unjustly treated.* This situation arises because all or *at all events* most men, while they wish for what is noble, *in practice* choose what is profitable. It is noble to do good *to one's friends* with no idea of getting anything in return: *and many men will therefore adopt this attitude.* But it is profitable to receive benefits, *and at the prospect of profit many men find that their desires are too much for their original wish. The 'moral' type, then, is suitable only for good men, whose characters may be relied upon: it only gives rise to complaints because most people find themselves unable to live up to the required standard. The rules for our conduct in it are clear enough: at all events, there is no difficulty when one is in the position of the bene-factor—one simply has to make up one's mind about one's object before doing the service, and act accordingly.*

If, however, one has been laid under an obligation of this nature, one should, if one is able, make a return of the same value as the service one has received: *most people, as we have seen, will expect it.* And one should make it of one's own free will, *before one's benefactor causes un-pleasantness by demanding it.* One should not 'make a friend' of him against his will—*as one is doing if one assumes that he conferred the benefit in the spirit of a true friend, and therefore makes the return simply at one's leisure.* One should therefore assume that one made a mistake in the first place, and accepted the benefaction from a

source from which one should not have accepted it:
one should assume, in fact, that one's benefactor was
not a friend (*in the true sense of the term*), nor was he
acting as he did solely for the sake of doing so—*these
two are the only possible reasons for making a free gift, and
therefore the only conditions under which one should accept a
service as a free gift.* One should therefore dissolve the
association as one would if the benefaction had been
made on fixed terms, *by making a return of equivalent
value. We provided above that the return is conditioned by
one's ability to make it: so in making the return 'as though
it were on fixed terms'*, one should return the amount that
(*if asked*) one would have agreed to pay if one could.
One can certainly assume that if terms had been agreed upon,
not even the benefactor would have expected to receive a return which one could not make.

Our general rule, then, *is that* if it is possible, one should
return the services rendered: *this will enable one at least
to avoid complaints of ingratitude. It is better still, of course,
to avoid all possibility of disputes: and this is simple enough.*
In the first place, one should examine who it is who is
conferring the benefaction, and under what conditions
he proposes to make it; so that one may accept the
benefaction under those conditions, *and abide by them,*
or decline it, *as one wills.*

*The repayment of benefits, however, gives rise to a further
question, which in fact concerns all cases where the terms of
the return are not fixed.* There is room for difference of
opinion as to whether one should take the benefit
which actually accrues to the recipient as the standard

by which to make the return, or whether it is the amount which the service cost the donor which should be the standard. *In fact, disputes frequently arise from this cause.* Those who have received the benefit say that what they got from their benefactors was a small thing to the benefactors; and they could have got it from other sources, *if they had cared to. In fact,* they belittle the matter. The benefactors go in the other direction: they say that the benefit was the most valuable of their possessions: it could not have been obtained from anyone else; and it relieved the recipient of danger, or some such stress. *In fact, they try to raise the value of the service as much as the recipients try to lower it. What, then, should be our guide in such questions?*

May we say that when the friendship is based on utility the benefit which actually accrues to the recipient is the standard *by which the service should be assessed? This certainly seems fair.* It is the recipient whose need gave rise to the action, and the donor fulfils his need in expectation of receiving a like return. It follows, then, that the assistance rendered is to be valued at the amount that the recipient was helped by it: and therefore he should return as much as he actually got—or *perhaps we should say that he should* even *return* more than he got, as it is nobler *to confer benefits than to receive them.*

In the friendship that is based on virtue, there is, *as we have seen,* no room for complaints: but *this problem does present itself when one party confers a benefit upon the other. And here* it seems that the standard should be the purpose of the benefactor: the determining factor in virtue—that is to say, in a good man's character—lies in the deliberate choice of his actions. *As the benefactor, then, chose this action deliberately in preference to others, as being of value in itself, it is right to judge the value of the benefit by his purpose in conferring it.*

XIV

We may now turn to the 'friendships of superiority', and see what practical issues are involved in them. Quarrels occur in the friendships of superiority as well *as in the friendships of equality which we have just examined: in fact, they give rise to quarrels even more easily. For whereas in the friendships of equality it is usually the action of only one party which leads to disputes, in the friendships of superiority* each party claims to get more *from the friendship than the other:* and when this happens, *they are bound to quarrel, and* the friendship—*in all senses of the term*—is dissolved.

Let us see, then, what the claims of each amount to. We need not discuss the friendship that is based on pleasure: disputes have no more reason to occur in this type of friendship when it is between unequals than when it is between equals. We are therefore left with the friendships based on virtue and utility. To take the claims of the superior party first:—

In the friendship that is based on virtue, the better man thinks it right that he should get more *than his partner: in every sphere,* the good man is awarded more *than the bad.* And similarly, *in the friendship that is based on utility,* the more useful man *claims to get more.* They (*the more useful parties*) say that it is not right that one who is useless should get an equal share *with one who is useful:* it amounts to gratuitous public service *on their part,* not friendship, if the results of the friendship are not to be apportioned according to the value of the services rendered. *In both types of friendship, where the superior parties argue thus*, it is because they think that just as in a business partnership[1] those who contribute more take more, so it should be in friendship: *the superior contributes more, and should therefore get more.*

As for the claims of the inferior party, the man who is needy (*in the friendship based on utility*) or inferior (*in the friendship based on virtue*) argues in the opposite direction. They argue that it is the part of a good friend to come to the aid of the needy: *let the superior party, then, behave like a friend, and dispense freely of his wealth or of his virtue.* 'What is the use', they urge, 'of being friends with a good man or a powerful man, if one is to get nothing by it?'

We need not examine the strict logical details of these claims: they are bound to conflict, and yet they both appear to rest upon principles which can be justified in fact. It seems, at all events, that each of the pair is justified in his claim, that is to say, that we should award more from the friendship to each of them—but not more of the same thing, *for that is obviously impossible:* the superior should have more honour, the needy more profit, *and thus both can be satisfied.* For honour is the due reward of virtue (*i.e. of a man who is good in himself*) and of beneficence (*i.e. of a man who is useful to others*), *so that in both types of friendship the superior should receive more honour:* whilst the assistance proper to need is material profit, *so that in the friendship based on utility the inferior party should obtain more profit—in the friendship based on virtue he will be helped in the direction of virtue.*

---

[1] κοινωνία: 'community'.

*We may perhaps gain a clearer insight into this principle
if we examine its working in a concrete example—that of the
political community:* this principle seems to be operative
in the constitutions (*not, of course, in the 'deflections', but
in the true forms*). *In public life,* the citizen who contributes nothing of value to the common wealth receives no honour: for it is the common property that
is given to the man who benefits the commonwealth,
and honour is part of the common property—*i.e. it is
awarded by the action of the citizens in common—so that
honour is given to the man who benefits the commonwealth.
He is given honour, not money, because in a properly constituted state,* it is not possible to make money out of the
common store and be honoured at the same time, *and
he, so far from gaining, loses financially by the benefits which
ex hypothesi he confers: but he must have some return, because*
no one can put up with having the lesser share all
round, *and as it cannot be money, it must be honour.* And
therefore to the man who loses money *by holding office*
the citizens award honour, while to the man who takes
bribes they award *the* money *which he makes, and not
honour. By this reason every citizen gets what he deserves,
and the state is preserved:* for *in public life* it is the principle
of 'according to merit' which restores the equality *of
the citizens which is upset by the inequality of their services
to the state:* and *the restoration of equality,* as has been
pointed out, preserves the friendship *between the citizens
—we must bear in mind that in a properly constituted state
the bond uniting the citizens is friendship.*

This principle *of 'according to merit',* then, should

govern the intercourse between unequals *in friendship
in general. In practice,* that is to say, the one who is
helped in the direction of money (*in the friendship based
on utility*) or of virtue (*in the friendship based on virtue*)
should render honour to his benefactor: *for* he should
render what he can, *and honour is all that he can give.
A strict application of the principle of 'according to merit'
would, it is true, demand that he requite his benefactor in kind:
but a friend is satisfied if he returns what he can.* For friendship does not exact what is according to *the* merit *of
the superior strictly, as justice does,* but what is possible *for
the inferior to provide.*

Indeed, it is not even possible in all cases *to do
justice to the merit of our superiors by the honour which we
render to them.* We may instance the honours paid to the
gods and to parents; no one could ever render to them
the equivalent *of what we get from them,* and yet the man
who tends them to the best of his ability is held to be a
good man.

This, *we may note,* is the reason why it would not
seem to be permissible for a son to disown his father,
whereas it is permissible for a father to disown his son.
A debtor should always repay his debts; and the son
can never, by anything he does, have done as much as
he has received from his father, so that he is always in
debt *to his father, and must continue to try to pay off the
debt.* On the other hand, it is permissible for those to
whom a debt is owing to renounce the debt: so that the
father may in this instance renounce the debt *by dis-
owning his son.*

We may add, perhaps, *that* at the same time it does not seem that any father ever would çut himself off from his son unless the latter were excessively vicious. Apart from the natural friendship *between father and son, which means that such renunciation would be a violation of the father's own natural instincts*, it is human nature not to reject the assistance *which the son will otherwise render to his father in his old age. It is natural, then, that such renunciations should not be common: and yet, if the son is really vicious, the father might as well disown him, for he can expect little return for his pains.* If the son is vicious, assisting his father is just the thing that he will avoid, or at least not be zealous about doing: for most people wish to have good done to them, *so that the son will accept his father's services*, whereas doing good to others they avoid as being unprofitable—*a vicious man, of course, will go to any lengths to avoid it.*

So much for these topics. *We may now see what practical issues arise in those friendships wherein the friends exchange things specifically different, such as profit and pleasure. In view of this characteristic of the lovables involved in them, we may style these friendships 'heterogeneous'.*

THE NICOMACHEAN ETHICS

Book IX

I

In all 'heterogeneous' friendships it is *the observance of* proportion which, as has been pointed out *in our discussion of such exchanges under the head of justice*, preserves equality *between the parties*, and *therefore* maintains the friendship. For example, in the community of the city, *each member has something different to contribute: and yet all are held together in friendship, because* the shoemaker gets in exchange for his shoes something in accordance with their value, and so do the weaver and the other craftsmen. *Each man obtains a return in proportion to the value of his product, and equality is thus maintained.*

Now in the community of the city, *the exchange of things which differ specifically is a simple matter, because* there is provided a common measure, namely money: and therefore everything is referred to this standard and measured by this, *so that there is no difficulty in assessing the value of different things in terms of money, and effecting an exchange through this medium. But in the community of ordinary friendship, there is no such common measure for the exchange of things differing specifically: it is therefore only to be expected that in this type of friendship disputes should be frequent. An example will show how they arise.*

In the community of lovers, *quarrels are notoriously*

frequent; and complaints may arise from either of the parties.
Sometimes it is the lover, who complains that he loves
his beloved to distraction, and gets no affection in
return—perhaps because he has nothing lovable about
him, *so that the beloved has in fact no reason to return his
affection:* and often it is the beloved, who complains
that the lover promised him everything beforehand,
and now, *when he has enjoyed the beloved's favours,* does not
fulfil any of his promises. Such situations arise when
the lover's motive in loving his beloved is pleasure, and
the beloved's motive in loving his lover is utility, and
they do not both possess these attributes (*pleasantness
and utility*). *One of them is then bound to be disappointed,
and they will quarrel.* For since these things form the
motive for the existence of the friendship, the friendship
is dissolved when the parties do not obtain the things
which were the reason why they loved one another.
The reason is that it was not one another that they
loved, but one another's attributes: and these attributes,
*as we saw in our preliminary discussion of the object of friend-
ship,* are not lasting; which is the reason why the
friendships *of lovers* are themselves *notoriously* transitory.

(*We may add,* however, *lest our picture appear unduly
gloomy, that* the friendship *of lovers* which is based on
character, since it is directed to the lovers themselves,
not to their transitory attributes, is lasting: this has been
pointed out *in our previous mention of the friendship of
lovers, and need not be discussed further.*)

*We can see, then, how easy it is in heterogeneous friendships
for one party to get no return at all for his contribution: but*

this is not the only cause of the quarrels which occur in this type of friendship. Quarrels also occur when the parties *do indeed get something from the friendship, but* get something different—something, that is, which is not what they were aiming at: for it is like getting nothing, when a man does not get what he is aiming at—*it makes no difference that he has got something, if that something is not what he wanted.*

We may illustrate this point by the *well-known* story of the promise made *by the tyrant* to the lyre-player. He promised that the better he sang, the more he should have: and when in the morning the lyre-player asked for the fulfilment of his promises, the tyrant said that *the lyre-player had had the pleasure of anticipating wealth, so that* he had repaid him pleasure for pleasure. If, then, pleasure had been what each of them wanted, all would have been well: but if, *as was actually the case,* the one wanted pleasure and the other gain, and the one *who wanted pleasure* has it, while the other, *who wanted gain,* has not got it, *but has got pleasure instead,* the terms of the community¹ cannot be properly fulfilled. The reason is, *that in all cases of exchange,* it is upon what a man actually needs that he sets his mind, and it is for the sake of this that he is prepared to give what he does: *so that if he does not obtain it, he has a right to complain.*

It is plain, then, that the return should be of what the man wants: but where there is no common measure, there is an obvious difficulty in assessing the amount to be returned. Which

¹ κοινωνία: 'association'.

of the two is to fix the value *of the original service*—the one who has conferred the original benefit, or the one who has received it? *It would seem that it is for the latter to assess it:* for the one who confers the benefit seems *by the very act of doing so without stipulating for a fixed return* to leave it to him. *There is warrant for this idea in the actions of a great man: for* this, we are told, is what Protagoras used to do. Whenever he gave lessons in any subject, *he did not exact a fixed fee; but* he used to tell his pupil, when he had learnt whatever it might be, to assess how much he thought his knowledge was worth, and used to accept this sum.

But this practice does not command universal assent: there are some people who in cases of this sort, *where things differing in kind are exchanged,* hold to the maxim *of Hesiod,* 'Let a friend's reward be stated and sure'. *Even between friends, these people would have the terms of an exchange fixed beforehand.*

This will certainly avoid all difficulties, provided that the agreement is kept: but unfortunately it is not always kept. Those who take the fee in advance, and then do none of the things that they said they would do, because of the extravagance of their promises (*which it is quite beyond their power to fulfil, though in order to get what they want people will make such promises*), naturally meet with complaints: for they do not fulfil what they agreed upon—*a promise should be as binding as an agreement.*

Some old friends of ours may serve to illustrate the taking of fees in advance: perhaps the reason why the sophists do this is because they are forced to by the fact that no one would give good money for what they know. *They have to get their fees before their pupils find out what their lessons really are: and their pupils have a right to complain, seeing that they paid to be taught wisdom.*

Even where there is an agreement as to the amount of the return to be made, then, people do not always agree about repaying it. We have seen that these persons who do not do what they have taken the reward for doing naturally meet with complaints. *We may now turn to those cases where there is no stated agreement.*

Of the cases in which there is no agreement as to the service *to be returned, we may eliminate from our discussion one class, in which no difficulties can occur.* Those who confer the original benefit for their friends' sakes, *and not for the hope of obtaining any return*, as we have said before, have no complaint to make: *such conduct, as we have seen, can only occur in the friendship that is based on virtue; and, as we know,* it is characteristic of the friendship that is based on virtue that it does not admit of complaints. And *when we have received a benefit from such a person*, we should make the return in accordance with the purpose *of our benefactor, not in accordance with the actual benefit that we receive:* for it is the purpose that is characteristic of a true friend, of virtue, that is to say, *as it is displayed in friendship. As his purpose, then, was simply to do us good, our return must be made in order to do him good.*

We may note here (in contradistinction to the relations of the sophists with their pupils) that this is the spirit in which it seems that we should make a return to those with whom we have studied philosophy. *They have conferred freely on us the greatest of blessings, and we must act accordingly.* The value *of the benefit received* is not *such that it can be* measured in terms of money: and, *while it is therefore clear that we must give them honour,* no amount of honour could counterbalance it. But perhaps it is sufficient, as *we saw earlier* in the case of the honours due to the gods and to our parents, if we render them such honour as we can.

But in cases where the gift is not made in this spirit, but on the understanding that some return shall be made, *we have yet to decide how the return is to be assessed.* Perhaps we may say that, ideally speaking, the return should be that which both parties think is in accordance with the value *of the service: this is manifestly satisfactory.* But failing such agreement, it would seem to be not only inevitable (*for the benefactor cannot dictate what he shall receive in exchange*) that the one who has got the original service should fix the value *that he will return,* but also just. *He is only under an obligation to return as much as he has got: and only he can know this.* The amount of the assistance that he received, or the amount that he would have given to obtain the pleasure, constitutes the value to the recipient: and if the other receives this much in return he will have the value due from the recipient. *We shall see this more clearly if we examine an instance of exchange in everyday life.*

We may see that this does in fact happen in the case of things offered for sale: *the price is what the buyer is prepared to give, not what the seller would like to get.*

There is further evidence for the validity of this principle in the action of certain lawgivers. In some places there are laws forbidding processes at law for the enforcement of voluntary contracts, on the ground that when one has trusted a man to make a return, one should dissolve one's association with him on the same terms as one entered into it: the lawgiver thinks that the man who was left to make the return at his discretion has more right to fix its amount than the man who left it to him.

The reason *which underlies these cases that we have cited* is that those who have a thing and those who want to get it do not in most cases value it at the same amount. A man's own possessions, that is to say (*regarding the matter from our present point of view*) what he is prepared to give, always seem to him to be worth a great deal: and yet the exchange is made *not for this amount, but* for the amount which the man who is to receive the thing fixes—*otherwise, there can be no exchange.*

The just value of a service or thing, then, is its value to the recipient. We may make the reservation, however, *that* perhaps the value should be fixed, not at what the recipient thinks the thing worth when he has got it in his possession, but at the value which he set on it before he got it. *He would have been prepared to give that much for it, if he had been entering into a contract: and therefore where there is no contract he should return this much.*

II

Now that we have laid down the general rules to guide our conduct in the various types of friendship, we may pass to some more detailed questions of conduct; many of these have been debated in the past, and they are all such as frequently cause us embarrassment in our daily lives.

Further problems that may be raised are such as the following:—Ought a man to award everything to his father, and *therefore* obey him in all things? Or should he, when ill, obey the doctor *and not his father*, and elect as general *not his father but* a man of military skill? Similar questions are whether one should do a service to a friend in preference to a good man, and whether one should repay a debt of gratitude to a benefactor in preference to doing a service to a comrade—supposing, *in both cases*, that one cannot do both.

Now is it not true that it is far from easy to decide with accuracy such questions as these? The cases admit of many variations of all kinds, both in respect of importance and unimportance and of nobility and urgency: *it may, for instance, be a matter of extreme national importance that the best general be elected; or it may be that the best man we know, whom it would be an honour to help, is in trouble. We can vary the details indefinitely, so that it is impossible to give a single ruling that will cover all the possible variations of one case. We must be content, therefore, with a few remarks which may indicate the lines along which such questions should be decided.*

To take our examples:—We certainly owe a debt to our father which we can never repay: but that we ought not to pay everything to one person, is plain enough. *There are others whose knowledge and skill entitles them to our deference in their particular spheres.*

Again, we should as a rule repay the benefits conferred upon us in preference to doing favours to our comrades, in the same way (*and for the same reason*) as a man should repay a debt to the man to whom he owes it in preference to giving the money to his comrade.

And yet perhaps not even this rule is invariably binding: here is an example *of how the varying details of any given case impose varying duties upon us.* Should a man who has been ransomed from pirates ransom in return the man who ransomed him, no matter who the latter is, *and however small his claims on him may otherwise be—* or should he even (*to make the case still more extreme*) repay him the money when he is not in the hands of pirates at all, but is simply asking for his money back— or should he ransom his own father *in preference to doing either of these things? It looks as though he ought to ransom his father—still more so in the second case:* for it would seem that a man ought to ransom his father in preference even to himself, *let alone anyone else.*

As we have said before, then, as a general rule one should repay a debt, *whether of service or money:* but if the gift *that we could otherwise make* outweighs this consideration in respect of nobility or of urgency, we should incline in this direction.

There are, indeed, occasions when even repaying a benefit is less obligatory than it would appear, even when there is no outside consideration to enter into our calculations. For sometimes it is not even fair that one should requite the original benefit bestowed upon one: *this may well be the case,* when one man does good to another in the knowledge that he is a good man, *and will make a valuable ally,* while the other has to make the return to one whom he believes to be vicious, *and so undeserving of his friendship. Again we may take money matters as a guide to the principles of exchange in friendship.* For sometimes a man should not even lend money to a man who has once obliged him with a loan: he lent the money to a good man, because he expected that he would get it back, but the other does not expect to get it back from a villain, *and he is under no obligation to throw his money away.* If, then, this is so in truth, *and the man really is a villain,* his claim *for the return of a service* is not equal *to the request originally made to him:* and if it is not so, but the good men think it is so, they would not seem to be acting outrageously *in refusing the claim.*

We can see from this example, then, how, as the details of each case vary, our duty varies too. As we have often said, therefore, discussions concerning feelings and actions have just as much definiteness as their subject-matter. *We cannot lay down precise rules to cover every contingency, but must leave it to each individual to apply his principles to the circumstances of his daily life. With this proviso, we may venture a few remarks on the problems raised by the conflicting claims of friends.*

That we should not pay the same things to everyone, then, and that we should not (*to return to our example*) pay everything to our father—just as we do not sacrifice everything to Zeus, *though he is chief of the gods as our father is chief of our friends, but only the sacrifices proper to him*—is clear enough. And since, *as we can therefore see*, we must pay different things to our parents, our brothers, our comrades, and our benefactors, we must award to each of them what is their own, i.e. what is befitting to them.

We can see from actual practice how this works out: for this is what people actually seem to do. To weddings, for instance, they invite their kinsmen, *but not necessarily those of their friends who are not related to them:* the reason is that kinsmen share in the family, and therefore share in the affairs which concern the family. And again, they think that the kinsmen especially *of their friends* ought to attend funerals, for precisely the same reason, *namely that funerals concern the family.*

Let us pursue the principle further: it would seem that in the matter of nourishment, we ought especially *of our friends* to assist our parents—*for two reasons*, because we owe our own nourishment to them, *and should therefore repay them the debt*, and because it is more noble to assist the authors of our being in this direction than it is to help ourselves, *so that the deed is worth doing for the sake of its own intrinsic nobility.*

Honour, too (*as we have seen previously*), ought to be paid to our parents, just as it ought to be paid to the gods, but not every honour. It is not even the same honour that should be paid to our father as that which we owe to our mother: nor again should we pay him the honour that belongs to a wise man, or to a general, but that which is proper to a father: and similarly we should pay to our mother the honour proper to a mother. *Honour is due to all of these persons, in view of their superiority to us: but as their superiority rests in every case upon something different, so the honour due to each of them is different not only in degree but also in kind.*

Further, to everyone who is older than ourselves we should pay the honour that is due to them in virtue of their age, by rising to receive them, and finding seats for them, and so forth.

Toward our comrades and brothers, on the other hand (*we have remarked before that these friendships are parallel*), we should exercise freedom of speech, and share everything with them.

And to kinsmen, fellow-tribesmen, fellow-citizens, and all our other friends, we should always try to award what belongs to them in each case; and, *where their claims conflict*, to compare the attributes of each in respect of closeness, virtue and usefulness (*and, of course, pleasantness*), *in order to arrive at a fair decision.* Where the friends belong to the same type (*as, for instance, when we compare the claims of two kinsmen, or of two persons who are useful to us*), the comparison is easier: but where they belong to different types, it is more difficult. We should not, however, allow this difficulty to deter us, but should make our decisions as best we may in the existing circumstances.

III

A further problem *which frequently meets us in friendship* is whether or not we are to dissolve our friendship with those who do not remain the same. *Constancy in friend-ship has always been accepted as a most desirable thing: what, then, are we to do if our friend changes his nature? Is there ever any justification for changing our attitude toward a friend?*

May we not say that toward those who are friends for utility or pleasure, when they no longer possess these attributes, there is nothing outrageous in dis-solving the friendship? *As we know from our analysis of the object of friendship*, these persons were friends with the utility or the pleasure, *not really with one another:* and when these attributes are gone, it is reasonable that they should not love one another. *Provided that each recognizes the other's motive in the friendship, these cases need cause no difficulty.*

A man may reasonably complain *of his friend's con-duct*, however, if he has treated him as a friend for motives of utility or pleasure, but pretended that it was because of his character, *and then, when the other is prepared to be a loyal friend to him, abandons him as soon as his ulterior object is attained.* (This situation aptly illus-trates what we said at the beginning *of our discussion of the particular problems of friendship, namely* that most of the quarrels between friends occur *on occasions of this type*, when men imagine that they are friends on terms which are different from their real motives.) If a man makes a mistake, of course, and supposes that he is being loved for his character, when his friend in reality does nothing to suggest this, he must blame himself *when he is disappointed.* But when he is deceived by his friend's pretences, he has every right to complain against his deceiver: in fact this deceit merits reproach more than that of counterfeiting the currency, inasmuch as the wrong touches something more precious than a man's pocket.

Where the friendship is between two good men, of course, and they both continue in their goodness, there is no problem. But if we approve a man as good, *and so admit him to friendship on this basis,* and he becomes vicious (or even,[1] if we believe that he has become vicious), should we still love him? Perhaps we may say that it is not possible—if it be true that it is not everything that is lovable, but only the good. And[2] it is also wrong, for one ought not to be a lover of evil, *as one must be if one loves an evil man:* nor ought one to *allow oneself to* become like a bad man, *as we shall do if we frequent the company of bad men.* We have said before, *quoting the proverb in our review of previous ideas on friendship,* that like is friend to like: *and there is this much in the saying, that friends tend by sharing one another's pursuits to become alike.*

Should one, then, *as this seems to suggest,* dissolve the friendship at once? Or may we not *rather qualify this statement, and* say that we should not do so in all cases, but only toward those persons whose viciousness is

---

[1] ἤ Ald., Rm.   [2] Rm.'s text.

incurable? *Toward them, it would seem that we should do so:* but where our friends are capable of reform, our duty to assist them with regard to their character is more binding than our duty to assist them financially (*which is admittedly among the duties of friendship*), inasmuch as character is a more valuable thing than money, and belongs more nearly to friendship *in the true sense.*

Our highest duty, then, is to continue the friendship in the hope of reforming our friends. All the same, a man would not seem to be acting outrageously in dissolving the friendship *under these circumstances.* It was not in view of his friend's possessing the characteristic[1] which he has developed that he was friendly with him, *but in view of his possessing the virtue that he has now lost:* and so, when he has changed his characteristic, since *though he may effect some improvement* he cannot restore him *to the character which was the motive of the friendship,* he gives him up.

A similar problem arises from the difference in virtue between two friends when it is produced in the opposite way. Supposing that *two persons were friends, and that* one remained the same, while the other became better and *finally* surpassed his friend in virtue by a great deal, should the latter still use the former as a friend?

Surely he cannot. This becomes especially clear when the distance between the friends is very great. This may well happen, for instance, in the case of those who are friends in childhood: if one remained a child in mind when the other was a man of the highest develop-

---

[1] [τούτῳ] ᾗ Rm.

ment, how could they be friends? They would neither approve of the same things, nor feel pleasure and pain at the same things: nor again would they have these feelings *of approbation and pleasure* with regard to one another's characters. Without these things, as we know, they cannot be friends *either for pleasure or for virtue,* because they cannot spend their daily lives together. (We have spoken before of these matters—*the causes and necessity of friendly intercourse—and need not discuss them here.*)

Well, then, *in these cases where we have been forced to dissolve our friendship with anyone,* are we to behave toward him exactly as though he had never been our friend at all? *This seems unduly harsh.* Perhaps we should bear in mind our past intimacy with him: and *so,* just as we think that we ought to do favours to our friends in preference to strangers, we should award something to those who have been our friends, for the sake of the friendship that is past—except, *of course,* when it is excessive viciousness that causes the dissolution.

So much, then, for the practical questions arising from our relations with others in friendship.

IV

We have observed the characteristics of friendship which are usually accepted in ordinary life: but we have not enquired into the more ultimate question of how these characteristics have come to be accepted. An expression which was constantly used by one whom we all revere may perhaps throw some light upon this problem. He used to speak of a good man as being 'friendly with himself': we must therefore examine this expression and see how far it expresses a true conception of friendship.

The marks of friendship in its relation to our neighbours—the marks, that is to say, by whose presence cases of friendship are *commonly* defined *as such*—seem *on examination* to have been taken from our relations with ourselves. *These marks are five in number: we have met them before in the course of our discussion.* Men define a friend as

(*a*) one who wishes and does what is good (or what seems to him to be good) to another for the other man's sake, or

(*b*) one who wishes his friend to exist (i.e. live) for the friend's sake. (This is what mothers do toward their children: and friends do toward one another when they have come into conflict, *and so do not meet but do not abandon their friendly feelings for one another.*)

Others, again, define a friend as

(*c*) one who spends his time with another, and

(*d*) one who chooses the same things as another, or again

(*e*) one who shares his friend's griefs and joys. (This again is especially characteristic of mothers, *whose love for their children is so often taken as the standard of human affection.*)

These are the marks by one or another of which friendship is *usually* defined. *What, then, is their relation to the expression 'friendly with oneself'? The fact is, that* each of these marks is characteristic of the good man's relations with himself. (They are characteristic of the rest of mankind in their relations with themselves, precisely in so far as they fancy themselves good: but it seems that, as we have said before, the standard *by which we must direct our enquiries* in ethical questions is virtue, i.e. the good man, *so we may ignore the rest of mankind for the moment. It is noteworthy, however, that men have confirmed this doctrine of ours by taking the good man, not any chance person, to provide their standard in friendship.*) *Let us see, then, how each of these marks fits the good man's relations with himself.*

(*d*) The good man is of one mind with himself: that is to say, he desires the same things with all his soul— *there is no conflict between his desires and his judgement of what is good.*

(*a*) The good man, again,[1] wishes for himself what is good, i.e. what appears good to him (*which is in fact absolutely good*), and does it. (It is, *as we know*, characteristic of the good man that he *not only wishes but actually* works out what is good.) And *when we say that he wishes and does it for himself, we mean that* he does it for his own

[1] δὲ Rr.

sake: he does it for the sake of the intellectual part of his nature (*which is the part which directs his actions to the attainment of what is good*), and this is held to be the essential of a man.

(*b*) Again, the good man wishes himself to live, and to be preserved: and especially the element by virtue of which he thinks. *He wishes himself to live, because* to the good man existence is a good (*whereas to other people it is a doubtful blessing, since only the good man can enjoy happiness*), and every man wishes for himself what is good. And *he wishes himself to be preserved, because* no one would choose that he should become another, and that the other thing which he has become should have every good thing (for *instance, though* God has at this very moment what is absolutely good, *no one wishes to become God, because that would mean the extinction of his own personality, so that the happiness of the God created in his place would mean nothing to him*): on the contrary, he will choose to have every good thing while he remains just what he is. And it would seem that it is the intellectual part of a man (or this part in an especial degree), which is the man: *so that in wishing for the preservation of his intellectual part the good man is acting for his own sake.*

(*c*) And the good man wishes to spend his time in his own company. *We know that friendly intercourse depends for its existence upon the pleasure taken in the friend's company:* the good man takes pleasure in spending his time in his own company. The recollection of his past actions is delightful to him: his hopes[1] for the future,

---

[1] ⟨αἱ⟩ Rm.

too, are good, and good hopes are pleasant. *He has pleasure, then, whether he looks backward or forward to his own actions:* and *for objects of thought outside himself,* his mind provides a wealth of materials for contemplation—*the most pleasant of all occupations.*

(*e*) And the good man shares his griefs and joys with himself more than *he can possibly do with* anyone else. *For he is absolutely consistent with himself:* it is always the same things which cause him grief or joy, not one thing at one time and another at another—he is not, so to speak, given to repenting of his deeds, *for repentance means that an action which one formerly found pleasant has now become distasteful to one.*

All these marks, then, which are commonly used to designate friendship as it exists between two persons, are peculiarly characteristic of the good man's relations with himself. It is, therefore, because each of these marks belongs to the good man in his relations with himself, combined with the fact that the good man is related to his friend as he is to himself (a friend being, *as the saying goes,* another self), that friendship is held to consist in one or another of these marks and that friends (*to put the matter concretely*) are held to be persons who are characterized by these marks *in their relations with one another.*

Whether there is or is not such a thing as friendship for oneself, however (*though our words may seem to have implied its existence*), is a question we may dismiss for the moment, *as a thorough examination of it would take us too far. We may, however, say this much, that* it would seem that friendship for oneself exists exactly in so far as a man is two or more (*how far this is a true description of human personality, and not a mere metaphor, we need hardly discuss here*) : this conclusion is indicated both[1] by what we have said *concerning the good man's possession of the marks of friendship, which might well be taken to imply that a man may have friendship for himself as for an external object,* and by the fact that the highest pitch of friendship is likened to friendship for oneself, *inasmuch as popular language describes a true friend as a 'second self'.*

We have said that the marks of friendship belong to the good man's relations with himself: but the marks we have enumerated appear also to be characteristic of the majority of mankind, base as they are. May we say, then, that it is in so far as they approve of themselves— i.e. in so far as they imagine themselves to be good— that they partake of them? *The reservation seems necessary,* since no thoroughly base and impious persons possess them, or even appear to do so: *our everyday experience suggests that at least a belief in one's virtue is necessary before one can possess them. Let us, then, examine the persons whom we have described as base, and see whether the suggestion made above holds good.*

The marks are hardly characteristic even of the base, *in spite of their apparent possession of them which we noticed above: we may examine them seriatim, as before.*

(*d*) The base are at variance with themselves: that is to say, they desire one set of things, and wish for another. This is what the incontinent do: they *are led by their desires to* choose what is pleasant but harmful

---

[1] ἐκ ⟨τε⟩ τῶν: Bywater, *Cont.* p. 63.

instead of what they themselves believe to be good, *though their wish is for the latter.*

(*a*) Others, again (*who belong to the same moral type*), refrain through cowardice or idleness from doing what they believe to be in their best interests.

(*b*) Those, again, who have committed many grievous sins, and whose wickedness has brought upon them the hatred of the rest of mankind, actually shun life and destroy themselves.

(*c*) Again, the wicked look for companions with whom to spend their time, and shun their own society. The reason is that when they are alone, *if they turn their minds back to the past* they have many unpleasant memories, while *if they look forward* they expect similar experiences in the future: but when they are with others they forget *their thoughts, and can concentrate upon the pleasures of the moment.*

And *in short*, since they have no lovable qualities, they have no friendly feelings for themselves: *none of the marks of friendship are present in their relations with themselves.* And, therefore,

(*e*) the wicked do not share their griefs and joys with themselves, either: we mean that there is civil war in their souls, in the sense that one part of their nature because it is wicked grieves that it must refrain from certain things, while another *because it is good* rejoices that they do so, so that the two parts drag the man in opposite directions as though to tear him in half. If it be impossible for a man to feel pain and pleasure *with regard to the same object* at the same time, *as our words seem to imply that the incontinent do*, at all events it is true that a man of this type, *if he does take pleasure in anything*, very soon feels sorry that he felt the pleasure, and wishes that he had never acquired a taste for such things: for the base are full of repentance—*they are continually being reproached either by their desires or by their rational judgement. (In this, we may note, they differ not only from the good, but from the thoroughly wicked persons whom we noticed above, whose desires and moral judgement are alike depraved.)*

It is evident, then, that a base person cannot be on friendly terms even with himself (*we know that he cannot in the true sense be on friendly terms with anyone else*): and the reason is, *as we have seen*, that he has no lovable qualities—*he is neither good, useful, nor pleasant even to himself.*

If, then, such a state is too miserable to contemplate, *the moral for us is plain:* we must shun wickedness with all our power, and try to be good. That is the way both to be on friendly terms with ourselves, and to win the friendship of others.

V

*Two feelings which have always been associated in ethical
theory with friendship are goodwill*[1] *and concord.*[2] *We shall
do well, therefore, to examine them both, and to see precisely
wherein they consist, and in what relation they stand to
friendship. Goodwill may be taken first, and by comparing
it with friendship we shall be able to bring out its true nature:
it will be remembered that in establishing our preliminary
definition of friendship we accepted as a definition of goodwill
'the wishing of good to a person for that person's sake.'*

Goodwill is like friendship, but we cannot say that
it is identical with friendship. *There is an obvious difference between them, in that* we may have goodwill both
toward people whom we do not know, and without
their knowing it, whereas we cannot have friendship
under these conditions: this has been said before, *when
we pointed out the inadequacy of 'reciprocal goodwill' as a
definition of friendship for these very reasons. Goodwill, then,
requires the addition of something else to convert it into
friendship: can it, then, be identical with affection, the
emotion from which the disposition of friendship is formed?*

But goodwill is not identical with affection, either.
Goodwill does not imply intensity of feeling or the
desire for action, whereas both of these things are
necessary concomitants of affection. Further, affection
requires intimacy *if it is to come into existence at all,*
whereas goodwill may arise of a sudden. We may

---

[1] εὔνοια.   [2] ὁμόνοια.

instance the feeling which spectators have toward athletes: it is goodwill that they feel for them when they wish their favourites to do well, but they would not assist them by action in any way: as we said, in fact, they feel goodwill of a sudden, and their affection is *therefore* only surface deep.

Goodwill, then, seems to be the beginning of friendship, just as the pleasure of the eye is the beginning of love. No one is in love, unless he has first taken pleasure in the outward form of his beloved, but a man who is delighted by the appearance of another is not in love for all that: he is only in love when in addition *to the pleasure of the eye* he feels a yearning for his beloved when he is away from him, coupled with an eager desire for his presence. The parallel is just: men cannot be friends unless they have first felt goodwill for one another, but men who merely feel goodwill for someone are not for all that friends to them. They only wish good to those toward whom they feel the goodwill: *this is one mark of friends, certainly;* but they would not join with them to aid their actions, or put themselves to any inconvenience for them, *as a friend, of course, is prepared to do.*

And so, *since it is the activity of friendship which is lacking to it,* we might by a metaphorical use *of the term friendship* call it 'friendship lying fallow': and one might say that given time and intimacy it becomes friendship *in the true sense of the term.*

We cannot say, however, that it becomes the friendship which is based upon utility, or the friendship which is based upon pleasure: for it is not *anything which we can accurately call* goodwill that is aroused by pleasantness and usefulness, *but some less noble feeling—goodwill, as we know, being entirely disinterested in its motives. It is true that* a man who has received a benefit awards to his benefactor, as a return for the services that he has received, the goodwill that is due to him: and *it is true that in so doing,* he is doing what is just. *But it is only where his motives are disinterested that we can speak of goodwill in the strict sense.* A man who wishes another to fare well because he has hopes of attaining to prosperity by his assistance does not seem to have goodwill toward him, but rather toward himself, *since the good that he wishes to him is only a means to his own good.* (In just the same way, a man does not seem to be a friend *in the proper sense* to another, if it is for some purpose of his own that he courts him.)

Generally speaking, *in fact*, it is virtue—some kind of goodness, that is, when a man thinks another beautiful, brave, or the like, as we saw in the case of the athletes—that calls goodwill into being.

VI

We may now pass to the consideration of concord. Concord, too, seems to be a friendly feeling, *in the sense that it implies a definite element of friendship between the persons between whom it exists.*

And for that reason, *we may say at once that* it is not identical with unity of opinion, *with which it has been coupled in ethical discussion.* Unity of opinion may exist even between persons who do not know each other, *and therefore could not be styled friends: whereas concord, since it implies some degree of friendship, can only exist between persons who know each other.* Again, *unity of opinion may concern any subject, whereas* men do not say that people who are of one mind upon any and every subject are in a state of concord: they do not, for instance, use the term of those who are of one mind upon questions of astronomy, because concord on these subjects does not imply friendship at all. *What, then, are the subjects upon which agreement is termed concord?*

Men say that cities are in a state of concord, when the citizens are of one mind concerning what is expedient—that is to say, when they make a deliberate choice of the same things or (*to put the matter concretely*) when they carry out their common resolves. It is therefore practical issues with which concord is concerned: and of practical issues, those which are of importance, and in which both or all the parties may obtain the same degree of satisfaction: cities, that is to

say, are in a state of concord when all the citizens are
agreed *upon a measure—for instance*, that the public
offices be elective, or that an alliance be made with
Sparta, or that Pittacus should govern; *the last instance
is especially instructive, in that concord was only maintained*
when Pittacus was himself willing to govern, *and not
when he laid down his office in spite of the agreement of all
the rest of the citizens that he should continue in it.* When
each of the two parties wishes that he himself hold the
office in question, like the characters in the Phoenissae
of Euripides, there is civil strife, *not concord.* It is not
concord for each party to have the same idea, whatever
it may be, *as Eteocles and Polynices, for instance, both had
the idea of holding office:* concord is the holding of the
same idea with regard to the same person, as, for
instance, when the populace and the better classes both
have the idea that the best men should govern; it is
only in such a case *that the condition laid down above is
fulfilled*, that everybody obtains what they desire.

It seems *from what we have said*, then, that concord is
friendship in the political sense, *i.e. it is the name specifically given to friendship as it exists between the members of a
citizen body*, this being the sense in which the term is in
fact used: for it is concerned with what is expedient—
the practical issues, that is, which affect the conduct of
life, *and it is agreement upon these points which maintains
friendship between the citizens.*

Concord on these questions *depends upon the standard
of values recognized by each individual, and therefore* exists
among the good *alone.* The good have concord both

within themselves (*we need not here dispute the legitimacy of such an expression as this*) and with one another, since they stand, so to speak, on the same ground. Their wishes remain constantly fixed upon the same objects, and do not shift and sway like the changing currents of a strait, *so that they have no discord in their own minds:* and the object of their wishes is what is just and expedient, *upon which they are agreed*, and *therefore* they join together in the pursuit of these things *without dissension.* The bad, however, cannot possibly exist in a state of concord (except to a limited extent, precisely in the same way as their capacity for friendship is limited *to the extent to which they can aid one another in their base designs and pleasures*). They aim at getting more than their share of what is profitable, and take less than their share of the troubles and public services. And each man, since he wants these advantages for himself, spies on his neighbour and prevents him from getting them: *they know that* if they do not keep a watch upon each other the commonwealth goes to ruin, *since everyone takes from it what he can and gives nothing.* The result, therefore, is civil strife, *as is inevitable* when men try to force one another to do what is just, but are unwilling to do it themselves. *The moral for us is obvious.*

VII

We may pass to another much-discussed topic—one which throws a deeper light upon the origin and the nature of friendship. Benefactors are seen to have more love for those whom they have benefited than those who have been well treated have for those who have treated them well: this is felt to be a paradox, *in view of the recognized principle that the recipient owes a debt of affection to his benefactor;* and men question the reason for it. *Here is the solution which is most commonly given:—*

To most people it appears that *it happens because* the one party is in the position of a debtor, and the other in that of a creditor. They therefore *follow out this analogy, and* conclude that as in the case of monetary loans those who owe wish that the men to whom they owe the money did not exist, *so that they would not have to pay them,* while those who made the loan actually see to the safety of their debtors, *so that they may live to pay them;* so *in the case of friendly benefactions* the benefactors wish the recipients to exist, with the idea of having their favours returned, while the recipients are not anxious about making the return, *and therefore have no reason to wish for the continued existence of their benefactors.* (*Wishing a person to live, of course, is taken as showing some degree of friendship for him.*)

Epicharmus might perhaps say that the advocates of this theory were 'looking at things on the seamy side', *in assuming such base motives for human conduct.* And yet it is not untrue to the foibles of humanity: *it is unfortunately true that the majority of men do aim primarily at securing their own profit, and so* most people tend to forget[1] *what it is not to their advantage to remember,* and are *for the same reason* more desirous of being treated well than of treating others well.

This explanation, then, does account, superficially at least, for those whose motive for action is their own profit. But what of the more noble characters? Treating others well is really a sign of nobility of character: and we must therefore seek for an explanation which will account for the action of those whose motives in conferring benefits upon others are disinterested. We will assume, then, that the motives of the benefactors are disinterested: why should they love the recipients more than they are loved by them?

It would seem *on examination* that the *true* explanation is more deeply rooted in the nature of things *than the explanation we have just discussed:* the case[2] of those who have lent money is not even analogous *to the case we are discussing. The analogy breaks down because* men feel no affection for their debtors, but *merely* a wish for their preservation in order that they may obtain their return: whereas those who have treated others well feel friendship, or rather (*since the feeling is not reciprocated*) love[3] for those whom they have treated so, even if the latter are not useful to them in any respect, and cannot possibly become useful to them in the future. *The explanation we are seeking, then, must be something deeper*

---

[1] Rs.'s ἀγνώμονες is attractive.

[2] τὸ Bywater.   [3] ἀγαπῶσι (not ἐρῶσι).

than mere desire for profit. We may illustrate the point we
are making by the actions of craftsmen, which do offer a true
analogy.

This *disinterested affection* is, in fact, what happens in
the case of craftsmen: every one of them loves his own
handiwork more than he would be loved by the handiwork if it came alive. Perhaps we may say that this is
especially true of poets: their affection for their own
poems is tremendous—they love them as though they
were their children.

This, then, is the type to which the case of the benefactors is analogous. What they have treated well is
their handiwork: and therefore, *just like the craftsmen,*
they love this more than the handiwork loves the man
who made it, *i.e. more than the people they have treated well*
love them.

We have not, of course, explained why a man should love
his handiwork so pre-eminently. The explanation of this is
that existence is an object of choice, i.e. of love[1] to all
men. Now we exist in virtue of activity—i.e. in virtue
of living, which is defined as acting—*so that activity is*
lovable to all men. Now his handiwork is, in a sense, the
man who made it in activity: *so that his handiwork is lovable*
to every man. Therefore every man loves his handiwork;
and the reason, *as we have seen,* is that he loves existence.

Now this *love for one's own handiwork* is based on a
natural principle—the principle that the handiwork
manifests in activity what the man who made it is po-
tentially: *this was what we meant by 'in a sense' above. We*

---

[1] φιλητόν: 'a lovable'.

were right, then, in suspecting that the explanation of the pheno-
menon under discussion is deeply rooted in the nature of things.

A further explanation is that to the benefactor the
action of conferring the benefit is noble, so that he
takes pleasure in the object of the act—*the person to*
whom he did it—in whom he sees the realization of the nobility
which he pursues: whereas the man who has been well
treated sees no nobility for himself in his benefactor—
at the most, he sees in him his own profit; and what
is profitable is less pleasant—i.e. less lovable—*than the*
nobility which is realized in action.

In fact, the benefactor derives a great deal of pleasure from
his act: in this respect, he has a far stronger motive for loving
the recipient than the latter has for loving him. Pleasure may
be derived (*a*) from the activity of the present, or
(*b*) from the expectation of the future or (*c*) from the
memory of the past (the most pleasant of these things,
and likewise the most lovable—'*pleasant*' *may for our*
present purpose be taken as implying '*lovable*'—being the
activity). Now (*a*) for the man who has done the
kindness his handiwork is lasting, since nobility, *which*
he realizes in his deed, is long-lived, *and so the pleasure of*
the activity is, as it were, present to him for a long time: on
the other hand, the recipient's profit, *which as we saw*
is all that he derives from the benefaction, soon passes away.
(*b*) Again, the memory of noble deeds is pleasant,
whereas the memory of things that have been useful
to us is hardly pleasant at all, or at any rate is less so.
On these two counts, then, the balance of pleasure is strongly
in favour of the benefactor: however (*c*) with the anticipa-

tion the reverse seems to be the case—*it is more pleasant to anticipate what is profitable than what is noble.*

Again, *a further explanation is that* loving[1] is like doing, whereas being loved is like having something done to one. *We may expect to find, then, that a man who finds satisfaction in the overt activities of friendship will be more active in loving than one who is by nature passive. In considering pairs of friends,* therefore, *we find that* those who are superior in the action of well-doing exhibit also *the other activity of* affection—i.e. the marks of friendship (*well-wishing, etc.*)—*in a superior degree.*

Again, everyone has more affection for those things whose production has cost him pains: we may quote in evidence the *well-known* fact that those who have made their money think more of it than those who have inherited it. It seems *obvious* that being well treated costs no trouble, whereas treating others well does cost pains. *The benefactor, then, having taken pains over the recipient of his kindness, loves him for that very reason more than he is loved by him.*

(*Incidentally,* this *last principle* explains why mothers are fonder of their children *than fathers are:* it costs them more trouble to bring them to birth. A further reason is that they are more certain that the children are their own *handiwork than the fathers are.*)

This *last remark* might seem to apply also to the benefactors: *they are more certain that the recipients are their own handiwork than the recipients are of the exact origin of the profit they have received.*

[1] φίλησις.

VIII

So much, then, for the reason why we love those whom we have treated well. Here is another problem, which is concerned with the nature of loving: this too has been discussed in the past, and we have already touched on the fringe of it in an earlier chapter.

Doubts are also raised as to whether one ought to love oneself or other people best. *Both views have their supporters. Here is one side of the question:—*

Men censure those who are fondest of themselves; they call them 'selfish',[1] using the word as a term of reproach. Also, *and this really supplies the reason for the censure*, it is *generally* believed that a bad man does everything that he does for his own sake—the more so, the more vicious he is (it is therefore a common censure of a bad man that 'he does nothing unless he is forced to').[2] A good man, on the other hand, is held to do everything that he does because of what is noble—the more so, the better he is: that is to say (*applying the principle of nobility to the particular case of acts done in friendship*) he acts for the sake of his friends, and lets his own interest go.

*The other side is as follows:—*Facts are at variance with these principles; and this, *as we shall see*, is reasonable enough. Men say that one should love best one's

---

[1] φιλαύτους: 'lovers of self'.

[2] Dr R. G. Bury (*Proc. Camb. Phil. Soc.* CLXIII–V, 1937) reads ἐφ' ἑαυτοῦ = 'in his own interest', and transposes the whole clause to follow παρίησιν: the conjecture is attractive.

best friend: and a man's best friend, *according to the accepted opinion which we know so well*, is the man whose wishes for the man to whom he wishes good are for the man's sake, *not his own*, even if no one is to know *that he is acting so well*. These qualifications belong in the highest degree to a man's relations with himself—and so, indeed, do all the other marks by which men define a friend (we have said *in a previous chapter* that it is from a man's relations with himself that the marks of friendship in his relations with others are taken, *and we need discuss this point no further here*). *The conclusion is obvious— that a man is his own best friend, and should therefore love himself best.* The proverbs, too (*which of course we must always consider seriously*), all agree *with this conclusion:* for example, 'friends have one soul', 'the property of friends is common', 'equality is friendship', and 'the knee is nearer than the shin'. All these will apply best to a man's relations with himself; and the reason is that a man is his own best friend—*were he not, the proverbs would not apply.* The conclusion, then, *from the proverbs as well as from the facts*, is that a man should love himself best.

Since both these views, then,[1] are such as to inspire belief, the doubt as to which we are to follow is perfectly reasonable. *How, then, are we to decide between them?*

Perhaps the way to deal with such arguments as these is to establish distinctions between them—to define, that is to say, to what extent and in what particulars each set has the truth: *neither can be altogether*

[1] δή Bywater.

astray, and we may thus see what the truth of the matter really is. Perhaps, then, it will become plain to us, if we can grasp in what sense each side uses the term 'selfish'. *We will take the bad sense first:—*

Those who make it into a reproach call 'selfish' those persons who award to themselves the greater share in money, honours, and the pleasures of the body: *it is natural that the popular idea of selfishness should be concerned with these objects,* for these are the things which most people pursue, and to which, since they believe them to be the best things, they devote their energies (and, *since most people strive to obtain them, and they cannot all possess them at once,* this is why they are *called* 'the goods men fight for'). Those, then, who try to get more than their share with regard to these objects are in so doing paying service to their appetites—generally, in fact, to their emotions, i.e. to the irrational part of their souls, *which is satisfied by such objects as these:* now most people are of the type who do this: and this is why the appellation has gained the sense it has, i.e. it is from the baseness of the common form of selfishness.

There is justice, then, in the reproaches directed against those who are selfish in this way, *for they are pandering to the base part of their natures.* And that most people do call those who award such objects *as those we just mentioned* to themselves 'selfish', is plain enough: *we may see that it is so from an examination of the contrary case.*

If a man always devoted his energies to doing what is just—i.e. to securing that he himself did what is just

more than anyone else—or to acting temperately, or
to doing any other of the actions dictated by the virtues;
and (*to pass over the particular virtues to what is the end of
the virtues*) speaking generally, if a man were always to
secure for himself what is noble, no one would call
such a man selfish, or attach any blame to him.
*Securing what is noble means acting virtuously, and no one
is blamed for that : it is securing for oneself lower objects that
is called selfishness.*

And yet, *if we examine his actions from the point of view
which we indicated previously*, it would seem that such a
man is more selfish *than the base type.* At all events (*if
we take selfishness to be the awarding of goods to oneself*), he
awards to himself what is most noble, i.e. the greatest
goods: and *it is really himself that profits by his actions, and
not the persons who profit in a lower sense by his virtue, for* it
is the most sovereign part of himself to which *by acting
rightly* he is doing service, and which he obeys in everything. *That this is himself may be seen from three things:*—

Just as in a city, the sovereign is held to be the city
in the fullest sense, and in any composite whole *the
ruling part is held to be the whole in the fullest sense*, so in
a man, *the ruling part is held to be the man in the fullest
sense:* and so the man who loves this part of himself,
and does service to this part *more than to any other, is
loving himself, and* is selfish in the fullest sense.

Again, a man is said 'to be self-controlled' or 'to
lack self-control', according as his intellect does or
does not control his actions; which implies that the
intellect is each one of us. (*We may take it for the moment*

that it is the intellect which determines our choice of what is *noble, as it is certainly implied throughout by the view that* *we are expounding, and is near enough to the truth to serve* *our purpose.*)

Again, men think that they have acted in the fullest sense 'of themselves'—i.e. voluntarily—when they have acted in accordance with principle: *implying, as it is* *intellect that determines our principles, that the intellect is the* *man's self.*

It is plain, then, that it is the intellect that every man is, or *rather, to be accurate,* that he is more than anything else; and it is also plain that this is what the good man loves more than any other part of himself. And so we may conclude that he is selfish to a greater extent— *i.e. in a more true sense of the term*—than anyone else: but it is with a different type of selfishness from that of the man whose selfishness is made a reproach to him— he differs from him, in fact, by as much as living accord- ing to principle differs from living according to the dictates of one's emotions, or (*to put the same point in* *other words*) by as much as pursuing what is noble differs from pursuing[1] what a man thinks is profitable.

What, then, is the practical conclusion for us from all this? Everyone approves and praises those who devote their energies in an especial degree to noble actions: and if everyone vied with everyone else to attain what is noble, and exerted themselves to the full in doing the noblest actions, *the world would certainly be far better,* *both for the common interest and for the private interest of the*

[1] ὀρέγεσθαι [ἢ] τοῦ.

individual. In the common interest, all things would be as they ought to be, and individually each man would enjoy the greatest of goods—if it be true (*as we know it is*), that it is the nature of virtue to produce such blessings.

This, then, would be the result of the proper type of selfishness. So that the good man ought to be selfish: for by doing what is noble he will both derive benefit for himself, and be of *material* assistance to other people. A vicious man, on the other hand, ought not to be selfish: for since *selfishness for him means that* he follows base emotions, he will injure both himself and others *by practising it.*

The selfishness of the base, in fact, is not truly selfish: not only is it the love of those parts of a man which are not his true self, it does not even secure what is good for those who practise it. For the vicious man, there is a difference between what he ought to do and what he does: *and what he ought to do is what is good for him, which only his intellect could ascertain.* The good man, on the other hand, actually does what he ought to do. *It is following the guidance of the intellect that thus secures for the good man what is good:* all intellect, *in whatever form it is found,* chooses what is best for itself (*for the good man, of course, this is what is good absolutely*), and the good man obeys his intellect. *He, then, by his selfishness in doing what he ought to do, obtains what is really good.*

But his selfishness does not mean that other people are the losers. It is true of the good man, *as we saw that it is generally believed,* that he does a great deal for the sake of his friends, even to the extent of dying for them. He will give up to others money and honours—generally, in fact, the 'goods men fight for'—since by so doing he obtains for himself what is noble. The reason is that *he takes no great pleasure in them, but does take great pleasure in what is noble, and* he would prefer to have great pleasure for a short time to having a moderate amount of pleasure over a long space of time: and *so* he would rather live nobly for one year than live for many years just anyhow, or would rather do one great and noble deed than many deeds of little note. *Let us examine his actions:*—

Perhaps we may say that this is what happens to those who die for others: *it is a great and noble deed, but it means the end of other actions:* and therefore it is a great and noble thing that they choose for themselves.

Again, the good would give up money on condition that their friends should obtain more money. A good man will do this, because *it is a noble deed: so that* whereas his friend gets money, he gets what is noble: and therefore, *while he benefits his friend materially*, it is the greater good that he awards to himself.

It is the same in the matter of honours and offices: the good man will give up all these to his friend, because to do so is a noble and praiseworthy thing (*what is noble being the end of the virtues, while praise is what other people award to virtue*).

It is reasonable, therefore, that such a man as this, *whose selfishness leads him to actions such as those we have described*, should be held to be good, since *as we have seen* he chooses what is noble in preference to anything else, *and to do this is the sign of virtue.*

This does not mean, however, that he will always take for himself the overt actions which are commonly esteemed as noble. He may even give up actions to his friends, i.e. it may be nobler for him to be responsible for his friend's doing them than it would be for him to do them himself.

In all the actions which are the subject of praise, then (*i.e. in all the actions which are commonly held to be the outcome of virtue*), we can see that the good man awards to himself the greater share of what is noble: *the true selfishness, in fact, consists in acting virtuously.* This, then, as we have pointed out, is the right way to be selfish: the way in which most people are selfish is the wrong way. *Provided that it be the right self that we love, it is our duty to love ourselves most of all.*

IX

We have, of course, been assuming that the good man will have friends. In fact, part of our proof of the nobility of true selfishness depends upon this assumption. We have not shown in what way friends are necessary to him: and it may well be objected that one can act virtuously without friends at all. We must now ask ourselves, therefore, whether it is in fact true that friends are a necessary component of happiness. Naturally, this question too has been much debated in the past.

There is also debate as to whether the happy man will have need of friends or not. *It seems natural that if he is to be happy he should have friends: but the opposite view has been maintained. Let us therefore examine this view:—*

Men say that those who are supremely happy and *therefore are* self-sufficient have no need of friends. *Ex hypothesi*, they possess what is good: they are therefore sufficient to themselves, and therefore have no need of anything to make up their happiness. A friend, since he is 'another self', provides those things which a man cannot by his own self provide. *The conclusion is that a man who can by himself provide all that he needs for his happiness has no need of friends.* From this opinion comes the *much-quoted* saying *of Euripides' Orestes,* 'When fortune favours us, what need of friends?' *which admirably exemplifies this point of view.*

There are, however, several obvious objections which we may raise against this doctrine. (a) It seems absurd, when we are awarding everything that is good to the happy man, not to assign him friends, since the possession of friends is *commonly* held to be the greatest of the external goods.

(*b*) Again, if it be true, *as we believe that it is*, that it is the mark of a *true* friend that he prefers to do good *to others*, rather than to have good done to him, *and that the good man is the only true friend: then the good man, if he has friends, will wish to do good to them.* And if (*as again we believe to be the case*) it is characteristic of the good man and *a sign* of virtue to confer benefits upon others, and more noble (*as indeed it is commonly believed to be*) to do good to friends than to do good to strangers, then the good man, *in order to attain the nobility which his virtue demands*, will need *not only* people to receive his benefactions, *but friends*.

(This, *incidentally*, is the source of the further queries *which we encounter in ethical discussions*, as to whether a man needs friends more in good fortune or in bad fortune: it is argued both that in bad fortune a man needs people who will confer benefits on him, and that in good fortune men need people to whom they can do good—*in both cases, of course, the conclusion is that the need is for friends, and so the question readily admits of debate*.)

(*c*) Perhaps, too, we may say that it is absurd to make the supremely happy man a solitary. *To say that a supremely happy man can live a solitary life is contrary to the plain facts of human nature.* No one would choose to have all the goods *on condition that he should live absolutely* alone: the reason being that man is a political animal—

i.e. it is his nature to live in communities—and, *further*, is by nature given to passing his daily life in the company of others, *so that the need of the daily intimacy of friends is a natural one.* This also, then, *since he is a man*, applies to the happy man *whom it is the object of our present ethical enquiry to discover: for ex hypothesi* he has what is good by nature, and it is plain to see that it is preferable to spend one's days in the company of friends and of good men rather than to spend them in the company of strangers or men of ordinary stamp (*it follows, in fact, from the preceding argument that the society of good friends is a natural good, and this conclusion is further ratified by common sense*).

It follows, then, *from the arguments by which we have supported our three objections*, that the happy man has need of friends. *But though it is easy enough to contradict the opposite view, it is exceedingly widespread, and there must be some foundation for it. We shall do well, therefore, to follow the method of the previous chapter, and see if that will bring us to a fuller understanding of the truth.*

What, then, do the advocates of the first view mean, and in what particulars have they the truth? Can it be *that this view wins common acceptance* because most people, *as we have already seen*, think that those people who are useful to us are friends *in the proper sense of the term*? Now the supremely happy man, since he already possesses what is good, will *certainly* have no need of such persons *to supply him with the material goods of life:* nor, indeed, will he have need of *the other of the two 'lower' types of friend*, those whose friendship is based on pleasure (or *at all events* he will need them only to a small extent); for his life is pleasant *in itself*, and therefore has no need of pleasure from sources extraneous to itself. *In so far as the view we are discussing relates to the two 'lower' types of friendship, then, it is true: and it is in fact based upon the belief that these are the only types of friendship.* It is because the happy man has no need of such friends as these that it is believed that he has no need of friends at all.

But perhaps we may say *at once* that this conclusion is false: *there is another type of friendship, that which is based on virtue, so that the argument is certainly invalidated on logical grounds. But has this last type of friendship any part to play in the constitution of happiness? Let us examine the matter more closely, for on the answer to this question depends the justification of our lengthy treatment of friendship.*

We said at the commencement *of our entire enquiry* that happiness is an activity of some sort; and an activity, it is plain *from the nature of things*, comes into being *by the process of acting*, and does not belong to a person in the same way as a material possession—*it simply goes out of existence again when the man ceases to act. We may assume, further, that the contemplation of an activity is an essential part of the activity, so that the goodness or pleasantness of an activity implies also the goodness or pleasantness of the contemplation of that activity. We shall deal with this point shortly: for the moment, let us assume its truth.*

To resume:—If being happy consists in living—i.e. in being in activity—and the activity of the good man is, as we said at the commencement *of our enquiry*, good *absolutely* and *therefore* pleasant in itself, *then the activity, and the contemplation of the activity, of the good man is a component part of happiness:* and if what is 'one's own'[1] is also among those things which are pleasant, *then an activity, and the contemplation of an activity, which is 'his own' is pleasant to the good man:* if, again, we can contemplate our neighbours better than we can contemplate ourselves, i.e. if we can contemplate their actions better than we can contemplate our own actions, and the actions of good men who are their friends are pleasant to good men (as they are, since they possess both the qualities which are naturally good, *i.e. goodness and, since they are the actions of their friends, the quality of being 'their own'*) : then the supremely happy man will have need of such friends—if it be true, *as we have just proved*, that he deliberately chooses to contemplate actions which are both good and 'his own', and the actions of a good man who is his friend satisfy both these requirements.

Again, men *commonly* believe that the happy man must take pleasure in living: *so we must see whether the possession of good friends increases the pleasure of life.* Now life for a solitary is hard: for *living consists in activity, and* it is not easy to be continuously active by oneself. But it is more easy to be active in the company of other persons, and in relation to other persons: and therefore the activity *of life* will be more continuous *for the man who has good friends.* And *it will therefore bring the more pleasure, since* it is pleasant in itself (this condition being,

---

[1] οἰκεῖος.

as we know, necessary for the supremely happy man).
*It is pleasant in itself, because the possession of good friends
stimulates the activities proper to virtue: and* the good man,
because he is good, takes pleasure in *doing* the actions
which are in accordance with virtue, while he objects
to the actions which proceed from vice—in the same
way as a musical man takes pleasure in good tunes and
is pained by bad ones.

A further argument *for the necessity of good friends* is
that one might gain a sort of practice in virtue from
passing one's daily life in the company of good men:
*since they too will be engaged in virtuous activities, their
company will encourage and aid one to maintain and increase
one's own virtuous activities, and so to progress in virtue—*
just as Theognis says *in his famous line 'Good lessons from
the good'.*

*But these proofs do not really go to the root of the matter:
we must justify, or at least explain, our initial assumption
before we can say that we have proved our case. To do this,
we must go back to principles which are deeply rooted in the
nature of things.* If we examine the question in the light
of principles more deeply rooted in nature, it appears
that the good friend is by nature an object of choice
to the good man: for we have pointed out that what is
naturally good is good and pleasant in itself to the
good man, *so that what we have to prove is that the good
friend is a natural good. Our argument may be presented in
rough syllogistic form,*[1] *the separate steps being distinguished
by letters.*

[1] I follow Burnet's analysis.

A. Men define life in the case of the animals by the capacity of perception, in the case of men by the capacity of perception or *rather* thought. Now a capacity is referred to its activity, *in the sense that* the deciding factor (*the thing in virtue of which the capacity may properly be said to exist*) is the activity. It seems, then, that *human* life is properly *to be defined by the activity of* perception or thought.

B. Life belongs to the class of things that are good and pleasant in themselves, *i.e. good and pleasant to the good man:* for *a fully lived* life is determinate, and that which is determinate belongs to the nature of the good.

C. What is good by nature is good (*and pleasant*) to the good man: *life is good by nature (B); and therefore life is good and pleasant to the good man.* (*Incidentally*, this is why life seems *to the unreflecting* to be pleasant to all men: but we must not take *as our norm in ethical matters* a life that is vicious and corrupt, or a life that is spent in pain. *The good, as we know, is determinate: and* such a life as either of these is indeterminate, just as its attributes *of pain and vice* are indeterminate. *We know already that vice is indeterminate: and* the case concerning pain will be made clearer in the following *book.*)

D. *Life is good and pleasant to the good man (C): perception and thought are life (A): therefore perception and thought are good and pleasant to the good man.*

If life itself (*apart from the incidental advantages of being alive*) is good and pleasant (as it seems to be (E)—*in addition to the proof given in C*—from the additional fact that all men desire it, and especially the good and

happy—their way of life being the most worthy of
choice, and their existence *in consequence* the most
supremely happy, *they have obviously most reason to
desire it: and as what the good desire is good in itself, it
follows, as we said, that life is good in itself*): and if it be
true (*as we assumed previously in a general way, and now
state definitely as a fact*) that he who sees perceives that
he sees, and he who hears perceives that he hears,
and he who walks perceives that he walks, and similarly
(*to sum up our illustrations*) in the case of the other
activities there is something *in us* which perceives that
we are active, so that *if we perceive*, we perceive that we
perceive, and *if we think*, we think that we think: and
if to perceive that we perceive or think means to perceive that we exist (*as it must* (*F*), for existence was
defined as perception or thought), while to perceive
that one is alive is a thing pleasant in itself (*as it is*, for
(*G*) life is by nature a good (*B, E*), and to perceive
what is good present in oneself is pleasant), *from which
(*H*) it follows that to perceive that we perceive or think is a
thing pleasant in itself:*—if life, in fact,[1] *as we have proved*,
is a thing worthy of choice, and especially so to the
good (because existence is a good to them and *therefore*
pleasant, *which is so* because they take pleasure in
perceiving what is in itself good—*i.e. their activity of
perception or thought* (*D*)—present in themselves), and
the good man is related to his friend as he is to himself
(the friend being, *as the proverbs have it*, a second self),
then just as his own existence is a thing worthy of

---

[1] δή? Resumptive.

choice in every case to the good man, so is the existence
of his friend—or *if it be too much to say that it is so in
exactly the same degree*, it is so in almost the same degree.

Now his own existence, as we saw, was an object of
choice to the good man because he perceived that he
was good—*i.e. because he perceived that he was engaged in
good activities*—and because the perception of this is
pleasant in itself. He must, therefore, *if he is to be
related to his friend as he is to himself*, perceive the existence
of his friend, as well as his own existence, *as an activity
present to himself:* and this, *if the account we gave of the
good man's activities is correct*, will be realized in their
living together, i.e. in sharing in discussion and thought
(for this, *since living in the case of men means properly the
activity of thought*, would seem to be what living together
means in the case of men—not, as it does in the case
of cattle, grazing together).

*We have proved our case, then: the good man's life, pre-
cisely because it is the highest form of human activity, needs
the presence of good friends if it is to attain to its full blessed-
ness. To sum up our argument:*—If, then, existence is in
itself an object of choice to the supremely happy man,
because it is by nature good and pleasant, and the
existence of his friend is very much the same thing to
him *as his own existence*, then his friend, too, will be
among the objects of choice. Now he must, *if he is to
be supremely happy*, have present to him whatever is an
object of choice to him, or else he will be deficient in
this respect. The man who is to be happy will therefore
need good friends.

X

Good friends, then, are a necessity for complete happiness: and this leads us at once to another question which has been debated in previous ethical speculation. How many friends should one have?

Should a man, then, *since friends are a good thing,* make as many friends as possible? Or is it *not rather* the case that just as in the matter of guest-friendship the dictum *of Hesiod 'Be* neither a man of many guests nor yet a man of none' is *commonly* held to fit the case, so we may apply to friendship the principle that a man be neither friendless nor, again, possessed of an excessive number of friends? *Let us examine our three types of friendship, and see how far our principle will work.*

What we have said would seem *on examination* to fit admirably in the case of those with whom we are friends with a view to utility. *It might appear that the more people there are to do us service, the better it will be for us: but we must remember that services must be returned.* It is a grievous task to return the services of a large number of people; *even had we the will,* life is not long enough to perform the task. It follows, then, that more than are sufficient to supply the needs of our own life are superfluous; and that, *by taking up more of our time than is necessary in the lower kind of activities,* they are an obstacle to living nobly. We may therefore conclude that we have no need of them: *friendships of this*

*type are only a means to the necessities of life, and their
number is clearly to be limited by our needs.*

We can do with few, again, of those with whom we
are friends with a view to pleasure: *life is not to be
spent purely in the pursuit of pleasure*—like sweetening in
food, *too much of this type of friendship is clearly undesirable.*

*The two 'lower' types of friendship, then, are easily disposed
of: our principle fits them both. But what of the third type?
We are agreed that it is a noble thing, so the question is
hardly so easily settled.* As for the good, ought we to make
friends of as large [1] a number of them as possible? Or
is it *not rather* the case that there is a measure for the
number of friends, in the same way as there is a measure
for the number of a city? Out of ten men, for instance,
one could not make a city, while a city made up of a
hundred thousand men ceases to be a city. But *this
does not of course mean that there is a fixed number of men
which alone constitutes a city:* the particular number,
perhaps *we should add,* is not one definite number, but
any number lying between certain limits, which are
defined *as the maximum and minimum numbers which will
allow the city to fulfil its proper function.*

This lesson may be applied to friendship: and we may
conclude, therefore, that there is a definite number for
friends as well. *We can hardly define the number in the
downward direction, for obvious reasons: but we need some
determining mark by which to limit it in the upward direction.
For this, we may take the activity which we found to be that
proper to friendship:* and perhaps the right number of

---

[1] ⟨ὡς⟩ πλείστους Rs.

friends is the largest number in whose company a man can pass his daily life. *We may indeed take friendly intercourse as our determining mark,* for this seemed *to us in our earlier examination of the marks commonly accepted as indicative of friendship* to be the thing most typical of friends: and it is clear enough that one cannot possibly live in company with many people, and distribute oneself among them *so as to be a true friend to each of them, so that this test does provide a definite limit to the number of friends that we may have.*

A further reason *for limiting the number of our friends in this way* is that they too must be friends with one another, if they are all to spend their days in one another's company, *as they must obviously do if we are to spend our days with all of them:* and it is no easy matter for this condition to be satisfied among a large number of persons. *Here again, then, friendly intercourse supplies a clear indication of the limit which we must set to the number.*

Again, *friends must, as we know, share in one another's feelings: and* it is difficult to join in the joys and sorrows of many people as though they were our own. *This again, then, provides us with a mark by which we may limit the numbers of our friends:* for *if they are very numerous,* it will probably happen that we have to join in the pleasure of one and the grief of another at the same time—*a situation where the genuine sharing of our friends' feelings becomes manifestly impossible.*

Our three reasons point to the same conclusion. Perhaps, then, *we may say that* it is as well not to try to have as many friends as possible, but to have only so many as are sufficient to supply us with company in our daily life. The reason (*perhaps we may call this the true reason, inasmuch as it lies in the nature of man*) is that *apart from its desirability* it would not seem to be even possible for a man to be very friendly with many persons. *The strong emotion of affection which goes to make up true friendship cannot of its nature be extended to many objects at once.* This is why it would not seem to be possible, either, for a man to be in love with more than one person. *This seems a fairly obvious fact, which points to the conclusion which we have stated:* for the ideal of love is a kind of acme of friendship, and this, *as we know,* is directed toward one person *only.* *As the acme of friendship can be directed toward only one person,* it follows that the strong form *of friendship* can be directed toward a few *at most.*

We may refer further to the observed cases of friendship: this seems to be the case in actual fact. We do not find many people joined together *at once* in the friendship of comradeship, *where the bond of personal affection is very strong:* while the proverbial cases of friendship *which common opinion regards as exhibiting an almost superhuman ideal in this type of friendship* occur between pairs of friends.

What is the truth, then, about those who possess large numbers of friends? It does not look as though this is so fine a thing as some people believe. Those who have many friends—those people, we mean, who meet everybody as though they were their own *dear friends*—are *commonly* held to be friends with nobody, except in the political sense of the term: *our discussion of the friendship that obtains between fellow-citizens has made it clear that in this sense any citizen has many friends.* Such people are in fact called obsequious *by those who speak plainly: and we may agree with the popular verdict that they are no man's friends in the true sense of the term.*

To sum up:—In the political sense of the term, then, it is possible to be friends with many people, without being obsequious, and being a truly good man. But for the sake of virtue—i.e. *as we have seen*, for the friends' own sakes—it is not possible to have friendship toward many people: we must be satisfied if we find even a few friends of this type.

XI

Another question of practical importance to us, at which we glanced recently, is: As we do need friends, under what circumstances do we need them most? Is it in good fortune or in bad fortune that we have the greater need of friends?

The facts are as follows:—Men seek friends under both sets of circumstances. Those who are in bad fortune need assistance, *and therefore seek friends from whom they may obtain it:* while those who are in good fortune need companions for their daily life, and *also* people to receive their benefactions—*friends, of course, supply both these needs (the latter need should not surprise us,* for the prosperous, *unless they happen to be notably vicious,* do wish to confer benefits *on someone, and everyone prefers that the recipient of their kindness should be a friend).*

These facts, indeed, make the case clear: we do need friends under both sets of circumstances, but it is for different reasons. Friendship, then, is more necessary as a means in bad fortune (which is why, *as we said,* men need useful friends then—*i.e. as a means to recovering their prosperity):* while it is more noble—*i.e. more desirable as an end*—in good fortune (which is why *in prosperity* men seek good friends as well—*not simply friends*—since it is preferable both to confer benefits upon good men and to pass one's time in the company of good men).

A further reason *why men seek friends* is that the mere presence of friends (*apart from their virtue or utility*) is pleasant both (*a*) in good fortune and (*b*) in bad fortune. *Let us discuss their presence in bad fortune first:*—

(*b*) Sorrow is lightened when friends share our grief. (Hence the question might be raised as to how the relief is caused. Do they, *as the popular phrase implies, actually* share in our grief as though it were a burden; or is this idea false, the truth being that it is their presence, combined with the thought that they are sharing our grief, which by being pleasant makes our pain less? *But this question belongs properly to the study of pleasure and pain: so that* whether the relief is due to one of these reasons, or to some other cause, need not be considered here. At all events, it is an obvious fact that what we said *of the relief which friends afford* actually occurs.)

But *the matter will not rest here: it is not the case that the presence of our friends in our misfortune does nothing but alleviate our distress, though it is true that it has this general effect.* Their presence seems *in its effects* to be a sort of mixture *of various factors.* The mere sight of our friends is pleasant *at any time,* and especially so to the unfortunate: and *therefore* they assist us in some degree not to feel our pain. (The reason is that a friend tends to console us both by his expression and his words, if he is tactful, since *if he is a true friend* he knows our character—i.e. what will cause us pleasure and what will cause us pain—*and tempers his looks and his words accordingly.*) *So far, then, their presence causes us pleasure. If this were all, our conduct in such circumstances would be simple:* but *it is not, for if they are sincere, they will grieve*

at the sight of our misfortunes, and so cause us pain as well.
To see a friend pained by our own misfortunes is a
painful thing: for everyone avoids causing pain to his
friends, *precisely because the sight of a friend's grief is
painful.* This is why (*to illustrate our point by our own observation of human character*) those who have a manly
nature take care not to make their friends share their
grief: that is to say, unless such a man is excessively
indifferent to pain (*as there is a danger that this type of
character may be*), he will not endure the pain which his
friends have to suffer *if he shares his troubles with them:*
and (*to sum up*) generally speaking a manly nature
does not admit fellow-mourners to his sorrows, because
he himself is not given to mourning, *but to facing his
troubles.* On the other hand, weak women and men of
womanish type take pleasure in those who weep with
them, and like them as friends—i.e. because they share
their grief, *which is what they imagine a friend should do.*

(*The practical conclusion from this is easy to draw:* it is
obvious that in everything we must model ourselves
upon the better of the types set before us—*and it is
obvious in this case which of the two is the better.*)

(*a*) *The case of the presence of friends in our good fortune
is not complicated.* The presence of our friends in our
good fortune brings us both the pleasure of spending
our time with them and the pleasant thought that they
are pleased by our good things.

*Our need of friends, then, varies according to circumstances:
and our observations will enable us to draw some useful
practical lessons for our conduct toward our friends—we can*

*say in general when we ought to summon them to us and when
we ought to go to them. Obviously, we must avoid giving them
pain, and try to give them pleasure: and they take pleasure
in the sight of our good fortune.* Hence it would seem that
we ought to be forward in inviting our friends to share
our good fortune (for it is noble to wish to confer
benefits), and to be backward in inviting them to
share our misfortunes (for we ought to give them as
small a share of our evils as we can—hence the saying
'It is enough for me to be in trouble'). *If we are to
send for them when we are in trouble,* we should call them
in chiefly when they will assist us greatly at the cost
of small trouble to themselves.

As regards going to our friends, on the other hand,
perhaps we may say that it is the other way round: it
is fitting to go to those who are in bad fortune unasked,
i.e. to be 'forward' *in this direction, as we expressed it
above.* For it is a *true* friend's part[1] to do good *to his
friends,* and especially to those who need help and have
not asked for it:[2] for thus it is more noble for both
parties—and *so, where both are good,* more pleasant—
*since it makes clear the sincerity and disinterestedness of their
friendship.* In their good fortune, on the other hand,
the case is not quite so simple. We should be forward in
going to join them in their activities (for men do in
fact need their friends for this purpose, *since, as we said
before, a man cannot be active so continuously alone*): but we
should be slow in going to them to receive their kind-
nesses, since it is by no means noble to show oneself

---

[1] ⟨τὸ⟩ Rassow.   [2] [τὸ] Bywater.

forward in accepting assistance. (*Here we must utter a caution, for it may happen that they press us: and* perhaps we should take care to avoid incurring the suspicion of being a kill-joy, when we refuse their offers: for it does sometimes occur *that a man incurs this reproach, even from the best of motives.*)

Our discussion has led us away from our original question: but it has served to throw light upon many matters which are of daily importance to us. We may conclude, then, that the presence of our friends seems to be an object of choice under all circumstances.

XII

*Since this is so, we may further conclude that friends will seek
one another's company to as high a degree as possible.* Does it
not follow, then, that just as to lovers the sight *of their
beloved* is the thing they love most of all, and *therefore*
they prefer this sense above all the others, on the ground
that their love owes its existence and its origin to it,
so to friends living together is the object most supremely
worthy of choice, *on the ground that their friendship owes
its origin and its continuance to it?* The reason why *it does so*
is that friendship is a community, and *the terms of the
community of true friendship are that* a man is related to his
friend in exactly the same way as he is related to himself.
Now the perception that he himself exists is an object
of choice to a man, and therefore the perception that
his friend exists is an object of choice to him also (*this
of course we have proved previously*): and the activity of
this perception occurs in the course of their living
together, so that it is reasonable enough that friends
should pursue living together *as an object of choice.*

And *we do indeed see that friends live together.* Whatever
it is that existence means to every man, or, *in other words*,
whatever is the object for which men regard life as
worthy of choice—it is in this that they wish to spend
their time in company with their friends: *for reasons
which we have previously explained, they find that their enjoyment of the particular life they have chosen is enhanced by the
company of their friends.* This is why *we see* some drink

together, and others dice together, while others again practise athletic sports and hunt together, or study philosophy together: they all spend their days together in the pursuit of whichever of the good things of life they like best. For it is because they wish to live together with their friends that they occupy themselves with these things, *which to them constitute living*, i.e. they share in these things as much as they are able, *because this is what 'living together' means to each of them.*

Once again, then, let us draw the practical lesson from our words: for we must remember that it is the activities in which we engage every day which shape our character. And therefore the friendship of the base is vicious, since as they are unstable the pursuits in which they share are base *(so that their association is vicious in itself)*, and further since, as they grow like one another *through engaging in base occupations*, they grow vicious *(so that its effect upon their own character is bad)*. The friendship of the good, on the other hand, is good *in its effects*, and grows *better* as their intercourse grows closer *and they act more in concert*. And further *its effect upon their character is good, for* they seem to become better, by engaging in their *virtuous* activities and by correcting one another's faults: *their intercourse is bound to have this beneficial effect*, because they take the impress of those things in one another which please them. Hence comes the saying *of Theognis*, 'Good lessons from the good', *with which it is fitting that we conclude our lectures on friendship.*

So much, then, for friendship: we have next to treat of pleasure.

35316959R00116

Made in the USA
Middletown, DE
27 September 2016